W9-BJG-833

Thomas Cook

Travellers

GRAN CANARIA & TENERIFE

BY

NICK INMAN WITH PAUL MURPHY

Produced by
Thomas Cook Publishing

Written by Nick Inman with Paul Murphy

Photography by Jon Smith

Original design by Laburnum Technologies Pvt Ltd

Editing and page layout by
Cambridge Publishing Management Limited,
Unit 2 Burr Elm Court, Caldecote CB3 7NU
Series Editor: Karen Beaulah

Published by Thomas Cook Publishing
A division of Thomas Cook Tour Operations Limited

PO Box 227, The Thomas Cook Business Park, Units 15–16 Coningsby Road,
Peterborough PE3 8SB, United Kingdom
E-mail: books@thomascook.com
www.thomascookpublishing.com
Tel: +44 (0)1733 416477

ISBN: 1-841575-03-8

Text © 2005 Thomas Cook Publishing
Maps © 2005 Thomas Cook Publishing
First edition © 2005 Thomas Cook Publishing

Head of Thomas Cook Publishing: Chris Young
Project Editor: Linda Bass
Project Administrator: Michelle Warrington
DTP: Steven Collins

Printed and bound in Spain by: Grafo Industrias Gráficas, Basauri
Cover design by: Liz Lyons Design, Oxford
Front cover credits: Left © Jon Arnold Images/Alamy; centre © James Davis Photography/Alamy;
right © Robert Harding World Imagery/Getty Images.
Back cover credits: Left © Thomas Cook Tour Operations Limited; right © Thomas Cook Tour
Operations Limited.

C o n t e n t s

KEY TO MAPS

⭐ Start of walk/drive $277m$▲ Mountain

☼ Viewpoint   🏛 Museum

✈ Airport   ✝ Church

Introduction

The Canary Islands were born as an international holiday playground in the late 1950s. Since then they have entered the north European psyche as a synonym for winter sunshine. Every year they welcome around ten million visitors.

Bananas, a typical sight in Gran Canaria and Tenerife

Despite its popularity, however, few people have any real knowledge of the archipelago. Even naming the islands, beyond Gran Canaria and Tenerife, would be difficult for most. The Canaries are popular precisely because they provide simple 'sun and fun' holidays for great numbers of people, and this has led to some resorts being transformed into concrete jungles and pastiches of home-life culture. Yet, to typecast the whole of a diverse island group on the evidence of two or three of its resorts is as ridiculous as writing off all Spain for a deviant *costa* or two. Beyond the beaches there is much to be commended by even the sternest travel critic. The scenery on all these volcanic islands is spectacular: from soft green valleys to charred lunarscapes, from Arizona-like gorges to snowy peaks and Sahara-scale sand dunes. Out of Spain's thirteen Spanish national parks, three are on the islands covered in this book, giving the lie to anyone who thinks nature is secondary to tourism here.

Cultural, historical, and ethnic

*These islands enjoy a fortunate climate . . . they offer
not only good rich soil . . . but also wild fruits to nourish people
without work or effort . . . these are the
Elysian fields of which Homer sang.*

PLUTARCH

Life of Sertorius 1st–2nd century AD

features are admittedly limited, but there is more than enough to occupy the average two-week stay on the five westernmost Canary Islands. Caves of the original aboriginal inhabitants lie open to discovery, the cities have fine museums and galleries, and there are superb examples of Spanish Colonial architecture in towns untouched by tourism. Folk traditions and island heritage are also still very much alive – to see Canarios at their best, just catch a fiesta.

It's quite easy to sample the 'real' Canaries. Just get off the beach, drive away from the resorts, and look around you. You'll be pleasantly surprised at what lies beyond.

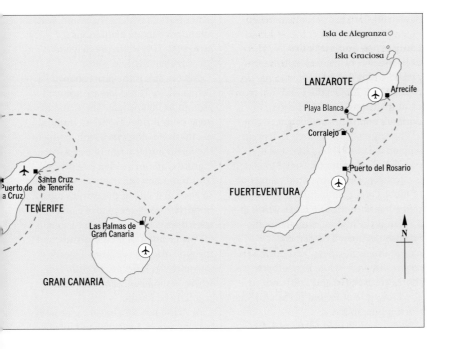

The Land

The Canary Islands comprise seven major and six very small islands, situated between 96km and 304km off the northwest coast of North Africa. This book covers the five westernmost islands: Gran Canaria, Tenerife, La Gomera, La Palma and El Hierro. Lanzarote and Fuerteventura are covered in a separate Thomas Cook *Travellers* guide.

Landscape near Fataga

For historical reasons the Canaries are Spanish territory, although the southern coast of Spain lies 1,120km to the north. Geographically, the Canaries actually belong to a larger island grouping known as Macaronesia (Blessed Islands), which comprises the Azores, Madeira, and Cape Verde islands. All of these volcanic islands have topographical and fauna and flora features in common.

Landscapes and statistics
Each island is of volcanic origin (*see pp8–9*) and is dotted with volcanic cones, either long extinct and overgrown or, as on Tenerife and La Palma, dormant and still smouldering.

The largest of the islands is Tenerife, with an area of 2,057sq km, and a population of approximately 813,000. It is effectively a great pyramid rising out of the sea and culminating in the snow-capped peak of Mount Teide, which at 3,718m is the highest mountain on Spanish territory. The island's mountainous northeast and northwest corners are lush, while its southern shores are parched and arid – not so good for agriculture but perfect for sun-worshipping tourists.

The round-shaped island of Gran Canaria covers 1,532sq km. It has the highest and most densely packed population (approximately 790,000) of any of the islands, two-thirds of whom live in the capital, Las Palmas. Gran Canaria is a classic volcanic cone in profile, with a series of mountains climbing towards a central peak of 1,949m (Pico de las Nieves). Like Tenerife, the north of the island, with its abundant banana plantations (*see pp90–1*) is wetter, cooler, and greener than the arid south.

Next in size is the heart-shaped La Palma where 728sq km are home to around 84,000 people. The island has a great central ridge (*cumbre*) running north–south along its length, rising in the north into the rim of a massive mature crater or *caldera* (*see pp8–9*). This mountain top protrudes into skies so clear that one of the world's most important complex of astronomical telescopes is located here. La Palma is by far the greenest of all the islands, and the only place (aside from Tenerife's Barranco del Infierno, *see pp104–5*) where natural running water can regularly be found.

At 378sq km, La Gomera is around half the size of La Palma and inhabited by just 21,200 people. Like Gran Canaria, it is a dome-shaped island and also has a north–south weather divide. At the centre is a plateau, almost continually covered in mist, with a dense laurel forest.

Last and the smallest is El Hierro, covering 277sq km, with a population of just 10,000. The westernmost of the group, and until the 15th century the boundary stone of the known world, it is a semi-circular sweeping curve of an island. Were the sea to be rolled back and the circle completed, a huge collapsed volcanic crater would be revealed. The landscape is green and varied, though not as dramatic as the other western islands.

Roques de García, Mount Teide National Park

Volcanoes

All the Canaries are volcanic islands, which are typically formed when molten rock and ash force their way up through the earth's core and the seabed to form a cone-shaped island, often scored by deep gullies (*barrancos*).

The first of the Canary Islands to be born was Fuerteventura, some 20 million years ago; Lanzarote appeared about four million years later, followed by Gran Canaria after another two to three million years. The rest of the group emerged over the course of the next 13 million years.

The nature of the volcanic scenery on each island depends on how recent and how extensive the eruptions were, and on the forces of erosion and nature's reclamation of the land. There are few places in the world as spectacular as the fantastic 'moonscapes' of Tenerife (only Hawaii and Iceland are comparable).

Here, cataclysmic events occurred very recently in geographical terms.

Tenerife's Mount Teide was blowing as Columbus passed in 1492, and there were further sizeable eruptions in 1604, 1605, 1704–5, 1706, 1798 and 1909. The most recent eruptions occurred on La Palma, in 1949 and 1971. These

were slight compared with earlier occasions. The explosion that formed the island's Caldera de Taburiente, some 400,000 years ago, was enormous – it is from here that the word *caldera* (volcanic crater) actually originates. One scientist has put forward the theory that another great eruption on La Palma could dislodge the western side of

Cumbre Vieja, creating a 650m high tidal wave that would set off across the Atlantic at 700km per hour.

Geologists will have a field day identifying the various volcanic rock types to be found almost everywhere, and with a little patience anyone can learn to recognise the most common of

them. As you tour the *malpais* (badlands) caused by the eruptions, you can see the three main types of volcanic debris: *picon* or lapilli (the tiny, light cinder particles sometimes put to good effect by Canarian farmers); pumice or *escoria* (small, lightweight, honeycombed rocks produced by the formation of gas bubbles in slow-

flowing lava); and volcanic 'bombs' (heavy, solid rocks, sometimes as big as footballs, with a brittle outer coat).

The lava, too, comes in distinct types. If it is the fast-flowing variety, it cools into rope-like coils and is known as *pahoe-pahoe* (the Hawaiian term for rope lava). The slower moving debris, which cools into slab-like folds, is known as pillow lava.

Tenerife's Mount Teide national park (*see pp96–9*) is certainly the most awe-inspiring stretch of volcanic scenery, but the most accessible is the Caldera de Bandama on Gran Canaria which can be admired from the adjacent viewpoint on the summit of the Pico de Bandama (*see p44*).

The volcanic landscape at Mount Teide (above and left) includes oddly-coloured lava. Opposite: the magnificent Caldera de Bandama on Gran Canaria

History and Governance

In 1982 the Canary Islands were granted autonomy (the right to self-government) as part of the general Spanish policy of decentralisation. Their government is conducted jointly from the two capitals of Las Palmas de Gran Canaria (for the eastern islands) and Santa Cruz de Tenerife (for the western islands). Las Palmas has been assigned half of the regional government departments and the islands' Supreme Court, while Santa Cruz has the other half of the departments and the Parliament. Each of the two provinces has a governor appointed by Madrid.

Guanche statue in
Candelaria

1st–2nd century BC	The Canaries are thought to be settled by a tribe with both Cro-Magnon and Mediterranean features, probably of Berber origin from North Africa and subsequently called Guanches (*see pp14–15*).		westernmost point of the known world.
		c. 1312	Genoese seafarer, Lanzalotto Malocello, lands on the island of Tytheroygatra. His motives and actions are unclear, but the island is later renamed Lanzarote.
25 BC–AD **23**	Ships reportedly arrive from the Roman colony of Mauritania, find native dogs, and name the islands (*see p24*).		
		1339–42	The first mention of Isla Canaria appears on maps. Spanish vessels are launched in search of the islands, though no conquests are recorded.
1st–2nd century AD	The Roman writer, Pliny the Elder, mentions the islands for the first time in his *Natural History*, calling them the Fortunate Isles. The islands are mapped by the Greek geographer, Ptolemy, who recognises El Hierro as the		
		Late 14th– 15th centuries	The Canaries come increasingly to the notice of European slave-traders and treasure-hunters. In 1402, the Norman baron, Jean de Béthencourt, with the help of Spanish nobleman

Gadifer de la Salle, sails under the flag of Henry III of Castile, intending to capture Gran Canaria and Tenerife. Instead, he occupies Lanzarote and begins colonisation.

1404–06 Using Lanzarote and Fuerteventura as staging posts for reinforcements, Béthencourt sails to El Hierro, where he tricks the small population into slavery. However, he meets strong armed resistance on La Gomera, Gran Canaria, and La Palma and returns to France.

1478–88 Ferdinand and Isabella of Spain order the second phase of the Conquest. A force led by Juan Réjon lands on Gran Canaria and founds Las

Palmas. After five years of bitter fighting, Gran Canaria is captured. After another five years, La Gomera is also subdued.

1492 Christopher Columbus uses the islands as a final staging post before his voyage to the New World (*see pp34–5*).

Columbus's model ship

1493	Alonso Fernández de Lugo lands on La Palma and completes its capture by stealth, tricking the last resisting chieftain into captivity.
1494	De Lugo's forces on Tenerife are routed in the Orotava Valley. But de Lugo returns to the valley with reinforcements and, following a bloody battle, the site is proclaimed La Victoria (Victory) in honour of the last battle of the Conquest.
16th–17th century	The islands use slave labour to gain economic wealth, first from sugar, then from wine.
Early 19th century	Cochineal, a red dye extracted from cactus-feeding insects, becomes the new island industry. This lasts until the advent of chemical dyes elsewhere in the world in the 1870s. Its collapse leads to large-scale emigration to South America.
1852	In order to stimulate the Canarian economy, Santa Cruz de Tenerife and Las Palmas de Gran Canaria are declared free-trade zones by Queen Isabella II, and become two of the world's busiest ports.
1880s	The first Canarian bananas are exported and become a mainstay of the islands' economy.
1936	General Francisco Franco, mistrusted by the Spanish government, is posted to Tenerife where he plans the military coup leading to the Spanish Civil War (1936–9). The islands quickly fall to his forces.
1960s	Tenerife and Gran Canaria embrace package tourism.
1971	The most recent volcanic eruption on the islands occurs on La Palma.
1982	The Canaries are made an autonomous region under the new post-Franco constitution.
1989	The Canary Islands, as part of Spain, become full members of the European Community (now EU).
21st century	The islands' tourist industry diversifies in an attempt to attract visitors away from the beach and into the countryside.

Garachico Castle, Tenerife

Representation and Structure

The Canarian Parliament comprises 15 members from Gran Canaria, 15 members from Tenerife, eight from La Palma, eight from Lanzarote, seven from Fuerteventura, four from La Gomera, and three from El Hierro.

In addition to its legislative role, the parliament sets island budgets and appoints representatives to present its case to the mainland.

Each island also has its own island council, known as the *Cabildo Insular*, which possesses certain powers of self-government and accepts responsibility for local services. These functions are in turn delegated to *municipios* (regional municipal units), then to town authorities, whose *ayuntamiento* (town hall) is usually a handsome traditional building in the central square.

The Independence Movement

The most obvious sign of Canarian discontent with the mainland is roadside graffiti spelling 'Spanish Go Home' or 'Godos Out'.

'Godos' (literally meaning 'Goths') refers to Spanish island workers, convenient scapegoats accused of taking jobs which should rightly belong to the locals. This does, of course, happen in some cases, but the 'Godos' also provide skills lost in previous bouts of emigration, when many able islanders went to South America in search of a better future.

The main regional party is the Coalición Canaria (CC), which carries around one-third of the popular vote. Its aims are moderate, directed more towards greater autonomy than towards full independence.

The term 'Guanche' meant 'native of Tenerife' in the original island language, but was subsequently used as a name for all the islanders who occupied the archipelago before the Spanish Conquest in the 15th century.

The Guanches almost certainly came from North Africa in the 1st or 2nd century BC, probably fleeing persecution, possibly in primitive boats. Little is known about their origins, and new theories and discoveries are frequently advanced. In appearance they were probably fair-skinned and sometimes blue-eyed and blond-haired (the Arabs did not colonise North Africa until much later).

There are no written records of the Guanches until the medieval voyages of Malocello (see p10) and the Spanish conquistadores. The Spanish discovered a people still living in the Stone Age: metals were unknown to them, and many Guanches still lived in caves, both natural and man-made. They were by no means savages, however. Some of the earliest Spanish journals praise them highly for their morality, courage, and intelligence.

Recent archaeological discoveries – particularly the pyramids of Güimar (see pp100–1) – are challenging previously accepted notions about the islands' original inhabitants.

The best indicators of Guanche life have been found in their tombs. Like the ancient Egyptians, they ritually embalmed their dead, and mummies and other finds are on display at the archaeological museums in Santa Cruz de Tenerife and Las Palmas de Gran Canaria. They also appear to have had a cryptic language of symbols, evidence of which has been found carved on rocks. So few have survived, however, that translation is extremely difficult.

When the Spanish arrived, most islands were divided into several chiefdoms or kingdoms (menceyatos), each ruled by a mencey who was advised by a council of elderly men. As elsewhere in the New World, the Spanish pursued a policy of divide and rule, making alliances with friendly kings, and encouraging Guanche to fight Guanche, until resistance was quelled. Aside from set-piece battles, however, the body count on both sides appears to have been relatively low, and the accidental introduction of European diseases probably killed more Guanches than did battle.

Life on the post-conquest islands varied. Many Guanches were enslaved; collaborators were well treated; a minority inter-married, and many were simply ignored by the new colonists. A significant number remained in hiding in the mountains, but many Guanches were coerced and intimidated by the Spanish Inquisition into 'abandoning their roots'.

Within a few decades, it is estimated that two-thirds of the indigenous people had disappeared, and within a century or so this ancient society had all but vanished.

Opposite: part of an exhibit on the Guanches at Mundo Aborigen, Gran Canaria
Above and left: relics of a lost people; a sign in Tenerife depicting Guanche statues, and Guanche remains in the Museo Canario in Las Palmas

Culture

The Canary Islands are a pot-pourri of many different cultures. On the larger islands you will find field workers and resort workers, cave-dwellers and city-dwellers, all within a few kilometres of each other. Yet many Canarios have never even left their islands, and the difference between Las Palmas and El Hierro is mind-boggling. What, then, is the cultural bond (if indeed there is such a thing) that holds this fragmented society together?

Promenade at
Los Cristianos, Tenerife

Guanche Culture

The Guanche language, dress, religion and other habits were extinguished by the conquistadores long ago (*see pp14–15*). Judging by the poor state of repair that Guanche sites are found in today, modern Canarios seem to have no great interest in their ancestors. This may partly be due to the absence of information about the first islanders, or may be because of Franco's policy of destroying any trace of pre-Spanish history on the islands, which makes it almost impossible to draw up a true picture of their society. There are still cave-dwellers today (at Chinamada on Tenerife, for example), but they probably have virtually nothing in common with their forebears.

Spanish Culture

The islanders may speak Spanish and look Spanish, but does this make them Spanish? A Las Palmas banker may say an emphatic yes to that; a farmer in a remote part of distant El Hierro may not be so sure. As post colonial settlements far from the mainland, with

a different climate and time zone, the Canary Islands were for many years 'the forgotten Spain' (although so were many rural regions in the mainland). Better transport and communications, the internet above all, have reduced psychological distances, but the islands are still in many ways a Spain apart.

Canarian separatism is often mooted and is the subject of popular graffiti, but true independence (as opposed to autonomy, a large measure of which the islands do enjoy) is not really on the nation's agenda. This situation is happily accepted by the Canarian banana-growers, who sell over 90 per cent of their crop to mainland Spain.

The popular images of Spanish culture, such as bullfighting and flamenco dancing, mean nothing to Canarios. Flamenco, originally from far away Andalucia, is staged only for tourists. Spanish *joie de vivre* at fiesta time is well embraced, however, and the Carnival celebrations on Tenerife are said to be the best outside Rio de Janeiro and New Orleans. Café life (*see pp154–55*), the siesta and football fervour are other shared Spanish passions.

Inter-island Rivalry

The two capitals of Las Palmas and Santa Cruz de Tenerife are forever competing to offer the best banks, the best port, the best cultural facilities and so on. For example, Las Palmas had to win a fierce battle for a second Canarian University to compete with that of La Laguna on Tenerife. The other islands are regarded as backwaters, and La Gomera, in particular, is frequently the butt of jokes.

New Influences

Tourism has inevitably had a major effect on many islanders. While those with businesses in the new resorts of Playa de Las Américas and Maspalomas have prospered and become the nouveau riche, many more islanders have been left behind. Youngsters have swapped a life of drudgery in the fields for working for low wages in foreign-owned hotels, while their communities, starved of new blood, slowly die. This is surely the worst of both worlds. Others, keen to develop their own communities to attract tourists, are either knowingly or unwittingly bulldozing their own heritage. Conservationists are now seeking to redress this balance and re-educate the people. The movement towards 'green' tourism, as evidenced by innumerable 'rural hotels' springing up, in the interiors of Tenerife and Gran Canaria, has proved that it is possible to create a service economy dependent on attracting visitors from outside without abandoning local pride, tradition and integrity.

Model of a cooper's workshop, Santa Cruz

Fiestas

Canarians love to let their hair down. In fact, to the visitor, it sometimes seems that island life is just one big round of parties – religious holidays, island patron saint days, village saint days, city foundation days, a day to celebrate the repulse of an English pirate attack, a day to mark the miraculous discovery of an image of the Virgin, and so on. Add to this the largest annual jamboree, the two-week *Carnaval*, and it's a fair bet that some time during your holiday you will bump into at least one fiesta.

BAJADAS

Aside from the Bajada de la Rama at Agaete, there are two other very important *bajadas* ('descents'). On La Palma, the Virgen de las Nieves (Virgin of the Snows) is brought down from her hermitage on 5 August once every five years to the island capital of Santa Cruz. A month of lively celebrations ensues. The next descent is in the year 2010.

On El Hierro the Virgen de los Reyes (Virgin of the Kings) descends from her forest sanctuary to Valverde on the first weekend in July, once every four years. Her next journey is in 2009.

Accommodation on both islands, scarce at the best of times, is much sought after during these periods.

Celebrations typically include a procession, either secular (marching bands and fancy costumes) or religious, depending upon the event. Sometimes it is a combination of both. The streets come alive with musicians, and food and drink vendors. Folk dancing, and sometimes Canarian wrestling (*see p152*) are staged. Fireworks often round off a fiesta, and revelries continue well into the small hours.

There are literally dozens of fiestas throughout the islands. Ask at the tourist office about local events during your stay. The most popular are listed below.

If you're not the sociable type or you value your sleep, then you may want to avoid certain places during Carnaval, and the

four- to five-yearly *Bajada* celebrations. Other fiestas are gentler, and should not disturb you unduly.

Carnaval (Carnival)
February
The big one (*see pp20–21*).

Semana Santa (Holy Week)
March–April
Hooded penitents progress through the streets.

Corpus Christi
May/June
This eight-day religious fiesta is the most important after *Carnaval*. The 'flower carpets' made in many towns and villages are the highlight. These are huge, colourful, pavement artworks (mostly floral or geometric, but sometimes in the form of an Old

Master), made of flower petals, coloured sand, or salt. La Orotava and La Laguna on Tenerife, and Las Palmas on Gran Canaria, are famous for their Corpus Christi carpets. These beautiful works of art are trampled underfoot by the devout during the procession.

If you are not on the islands during Corpus Christi, you may still be able to see a demonstration of 'sand-painting' at Casa de Los Balcones, La Orotava on Tenerife (*see p84*).

Romerías
June/July
A *romería* (pilgrimage) can be a most colourful celebration, particularly when the statue of the local Virgin is paraded through the streets on a highly decorated cart pulled by two dressed-up bullocks. There are two very good *romerías* on Tenerife: San Isidro at La Orotava in June, and San Benito Abad at La Laguna on the first Sunday in July.

Bajada de la Rama (Descent of the Branch)
4 August
This popular and joyful fiesta, held at Agaete, Gran Canaria, is derived from an ancient Guanche rain-making ritual.

Virgin de la Candelaria

Carnaval

Carnaval (Carnival) is the biggest, costliest, most frenzied and eagerly awaited event on the islands each year. As soon as one *Carnaval* is finished preparations begin for next year's extravaganza. It takes months to make some of the costumes, and the floats are often works of art. More than any other gesture, the huge sums of money spent on *Carnaval* by a people who are relatively poor, demonstrates their love of the fiesta.

Carnaval goes on for two hedonistic weeks with a programme of nightly outdoor dancing, usually to the hottest Latin American dance bands, fancy dress and drag competitions. Stalls selling *cubata* (rum and cola), *churros* (a type of Spanish doughnut), and *pinchitos* (kebabs) are everywhere.

Most of the big *Carnaval* attractions, called *cabalgatas*, take place at the weekend, so that people can lie in the day after celebrations. Many of the schools have their half-term at this time, so the smaller children can also have their fancy dress parties at school.

The highlight of all this activity is, of course, the main procession. Comparison with the famous Rio Carnival is obvious, and perhaps not surprising, given the number of Canarios who have emigrated to South America. Drummers beat out pulsating Latin rhythms, while the Carnival Queens stand proud on top of the procession floats in their magnificent dresses. The troupes alongside the floats, also in glitter, feathers, and often little else, rumba and samba along the procession route with the vitality and stamina of world-class athletes. Alongside them are drag queens, Charlie Chaplin and Fidel Castro look-alikes, plus a multitude of fancy-dressed children.

The *Murgas* are groups of men dressed alike in the costume theme of the year, who chant (rather like folklore rap) about various politicians or famous people and their 'gaffes'. In the past, when the government was more dictatorial, this was used as a form of satire against the various political institutions, without much risk of reprisal.

The most extraordinary sight during *Carnaval* is known as the Burial of the Sardine. An 8–10m-long cardboard/papier-mâché sardine is dragged to the harbour or the main square accompanied by mourners, invariably men dressed in black drag, theatrically 'weeping' and 'wailing' for all they are worth. At the appointed spot, fireworks inside the sardine are set off, and it literally blows itself apart. A grand firework display then follows.

The best places to catch *Carnaval* are Santa Cruz and Puerto de la Cruz on Tenerife, and Las Palmas on Gran Canaria. Dates vary. It starts first in Santa Cruz, ending on Ash Wednesday, then fans out to all other points and other islands. Enquire at the tourist office in advance.

The colourful parade at *Carnaval*, Puerto de la Cruz

Impressions

Over the last three decades, the Canary Islands have become as well known as the Spanish *costas* for a budget family playground of sun, sea, and sand. It is true that this type of holiday can be found in abundance in the southern resorts of Tenerife and Gran Canaria. But elsewhere on the islands there are few family tourism facilities, surprisingly little sand and, away from the southern shores, even the sun is not always reliable. All this means fewer people, which to some holidaymakers is an attraction in itself.

'The blue sky and all-pervading sun overhead, the delicious warmth but exquisite freshness of the air, all tell us that we have reached the haven of our rest … the Fortunate Islands.'

Ernest Hart *Letter to the British Medical Journal about Tenerife in 1887*

Which Island?

If you're the social type and like to be among people of your own nationality, drinking in the types of bars you find at home and with all facilities laid on, then the mega resorts in southern Tenerife and Gran Canaria are made for you. The highlights of all islands are well catered for by coach trips, so you don't even have to hire a car.

There's little to choose between the two islands in terms of overall appeal. The former takes the lead in terms of beaches; the latter has more man-made attractions to enjoy.

At the other extreme, if you're the solitary type who takes pleasure in lonely walks, landscapes, and quiet local bars, one of the minor islands may well be your scene (though even among these, El Hierro may be a little too quiet for most).

It's possible to get the best of both worlds by staying in a rural hotel in the centre or north of Gran Canaria or Tenerife from which you can reach the beach but which you can retreat back to when you feel the need for silence and a country walk. If you prefer a smaller island, there is a handful of luxury hotels on La Gomera and La Palma which make it easy to go native without giving up comforts or feeling too far from civilisation.

Island-hopping

There is no tradition of island-hopping travel in the Canaries, unlike the Greek Islands. This is partly due to the distances involved but mainly to the packaged nature of most Canarian holidays and the packaged image of the islands, which has attracted a less adventurous type of traveller. But there is everything to be gained by breaking the mould, and the obstacles to inter-island travel are more psychological than actual. Tenerife and La Gomera are easy to combine due to their proximity, and 35-minute sailing times and high-speed ferries link Tenerife with Gran Canaria. If you want to see several islands in the same trip, flying is the most painless way to get around. All islands have their own airport and it is possible to reach any island from any other in under 45 minutes' flying time. Fares are reasonable, check-in times are short, and it's an ideal way to sample the smaller islands for a day or two before committing yourself to a longer stay. Inter-island flights go via Gran Canaria for the eastern islands, and Tenerife (Los Rodeos, north airport) for the western islands. Car hire companies are used to dealing with clients visiting more than one island and there are now many good, mid-price hotels catering for people who create their own itineraries rather than stay put for a week in a package resort.

Tourism is big business in the Canary Islands, but the traditional way of life continues

The harbour at Agaete, Gran Canaria

Cultural Differences

If you're familiar with mainland Spain then you won't find too much to surprise you in the Canary Islands. Tourism is so well established on all the islands, except El Hierro, that you'll very rarely have a problem making yourself understood, or finding what you want. However, this doesn't mean that you should assume everyone speaks English. A little Spanish will always be appreciated, and it's essential if you want to order something that is not on view, or ask what's cooking in the kitchen. In village bars they don't always have menus, or even food on display, but they'll usually be pleased to cook you a snack.

Don't forget the old tradition of the long lunch break. Villages and towns close down from around 1pm until 4 or 5pm. This isn't a good time to explore any settlement, as churches, museums and shops will all be closed, and there will be a general ghost town atmosphere. It's much better to arrive in the early evening, when the Spanish tradition of the *paseo* (the promenade, or evening stroll) brings life back into the streets, and a lively atmosphere prevails in bars and cafés. When the paseo finishes, it is time to eat. The evening meal is generally taken around 8pm, a little later than in northern Europe, though early by Spanish mainland standards.

Puerto Rico, Gran Canaria

WHAT'S IN A NAME

Surprising as it may seem, the Canary Islands are not named after the tiny yellow finch-like bird that inhabits the islands. In fact, it is the reverse, the birds taking their name from the islands (they also live on the other Macaronesian islands, see p6). If you want to glimpse a rare canary in the wild, look among stands of Canary pines, though you'll have a much better chance of seeing them in cages outside village houses on Gran Canaria and Tenerife.

The most enduring legend associated with the name of the islands is that they were named after native dogs (*canes*, Spanish for canines) found by the early Mauretanian explorers. Today's *verdino*, the native Canarian dog, is presumed to be a descendant. If you don't see any real *verdinos*, look out for the famous statues by the cathedral in Las Palmas on Gran Canaria.

Copy the locals – take time to stop and rest

Gran Canaria

Despite its name and fame, Gran Canaria is not the biggest island of the Canaries (it is the third largest), yet somehow it feels big. Las Palmas is the most populous and dynamic city on the archipelago; Maspalomas is one of the largest resort complexes in Europe, and the inland scenery is grand in every sense. Only Tenerife can match its combination of cosmopolitan, rural and seaside attractions, but there is no question that the beaches of Gran Canaria are far superior.

The island's comparatively small size can also be an advantage. Both Las Palmas and Maspalomas are just 30 minutes from the airport, and no place on the island is more than an hour's drive from either of these destinations. In fact, it's possible to drive round the whole island in a day, but it will be a long day.

Gran Canaria is the most popular island after Tenerife, but if you do wish to get away from it all you needn't worry about tourist hordes. The majority of visitors simply flop on to their towels and stay there, although an increasing number of tourists are now exploring and staying in the quieter rural areas.

Gran Canaria is often called 'a continent in miniature', a reference to the extremes of landscape and climate that may be found on this island. Its landscapes change quickly from Wild West canyons to idyllic pine forests to Sahara-like dunes, and while there may be a dusting of snow on Pico de las Nieves, Maspalomas will still be wallowing in sun.

Gran Canaria is also culturally and historically the most well-endowed of the islands. A rich collection of Guanche sites and relics is scattered around, and the Canaries' best performing arts and museums are in Las Palmas.

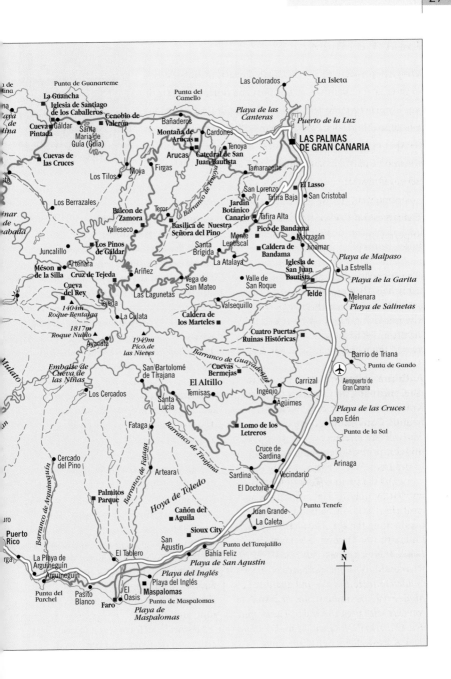

Las Palmas

With a population of 377,000, Las Palmas is the biggest city in the Canary Islands. A major port and business centre, it was also (before modern mass tourism got into its stride) a fashionable resort. Nowadays most holidaymakers head to the purpose-built southern developments, where sunshine is virtually guaranteed, and a 'real British pub' is never far away.

Catedral de Santa Ana

The city is not to everyone's taste. It is busy, noisy, run-down in parts and suffers from petty crime and traffic problems. But there is more Spanish atmosphere, history, and culture to enjoy here than anywhere else on the island.
Tourist office: León y Castilla, 322. Tel: (928) 446824. Open: Mon–Fri 9am–1.30pm & 5–7pm, Sat 9.30am–1pm.

Auditorio Alfredo Kraus & Palacio de Congresos de Canarias (Alfredo Kraus Auditorium and Canary Islands Convention Centre)

The work of architect Oscar Turquets, this comprises eleven sound-proofed chambers, seven of them bearing the names of the various Canary Islands, and the Symphony Hall, which has an enormous window behind the stage overlooking the sea. The Gran Canarian Philharmonic Orchestra is based here.
Playa de las Canteras, Tel: (928) 491770. www.auditorio-alfredokraus.com Guided tours in English and Spanish: Mon–Fri 12.00 midday, Sun 11.30am (to coincide with organ recitals). Ticket office: Tel: (902) 405504. Open: Mon–Fri 10am–2pm, 4.30–8.30pm, Sat 10am–2pm.

Catedral de Santa Ana (Cathedral of St Ana)

From the outside there is little to commend this huge, grimy building. Construction began in 1497, but it was still being built in the 20th century. Inside, however, there are many treasures. Its **Museo Diocesano de Arte Sacro** (Museum of Religious Art) boasts a rich collection of statues, paintings, and gold and silver ware.
Plaza de Santa Ana. Tel: (928) 313600. Museum: enter from Calle Espíritu Santo. Tel: (928) 314989. Open: Mon–Fri 10am–4.30pm, Sat 10am–1.30pm. Admission charge.

Parque Doramas/Pueblo Canario (Canary Village)

The centrepiece of this pleasant, grassy park is the Pueblo Canario, an idealised re-creation of a typical village, including a church, a *bodega* (wine bar), shops, a tourist office, and the **Museo de Néstor**, arranged around a pretty square. On Sunday mornings and Thursday evenings a folk group entertains with song and dance.

Néstor de la Torre was a famous local artist and designer who conceived,

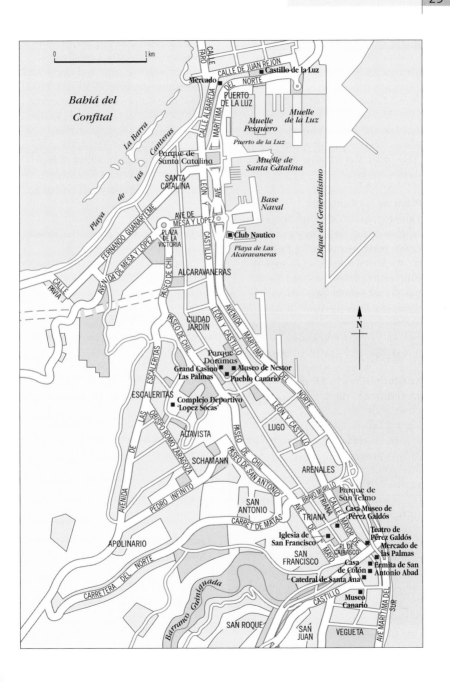

among other projects, the Pueblo Canario. The Museo de Néstor features many of his best exotic Symbolist paintings.

Pueblo Canario. Tel: (928) 245135. Open: Tue–Sat 10am–1pm, 4–8pm, Sun 10.30am–2.30pm. Admission charge. Museo Néstor. Open: Tue–Sat 10am–8pm, Sun 10.30am–2.30pm. Admission charge.

Playa de las Canteras

This long, golden, crescent-shaped beach is one of the longest city beaches in the world, extending for 2.6km on the northwest side of Las Palmas. It is conveniently protected from Atlantic rollers by a natural reef close to the shore, and is ideal for safe bathing.

Casa de Colón, detail

There are clean changing rooms, showers and toilets for a small fee. Those in search of wind and waves need only venture out beyond the reef. The promenade is lined with restaurants of many nationalities – Bulgarian, Korean, and Japanese sit alongside British, German, and Swedish eating houses, reflecting the home countries of the sailors who take 'rest and recreation' here alongside ordinary holidaymakers.

Puerto de la Luz

Las Palmas was once one of the busiest ports in the western hemisphere.

Today, it still throbs with activity with up to 1,000 ships a month passing through, but it has lost much of its vitality. The number of sailors has diminished as cargo-handling has become less labour-intensive, and few ocean liners now call here.

The port is at its most colourful on Sunday mornings, when the *rastro* (flea market) on the Avenida Marítima is patronised by locals, tourists, and a good number of West African shoppers and vendors. Nearby, in Calle de Juan Rejón, the sturdy stone **Castillo de la Luz** (castle), built in 1494, is the oldest building on Gran Canaria. It is occasionally open for special exhibitions.

Santa Catalina

This is the bustling area behind the beach, jam-packed with duty-free shops, hotels, restaurants, bars, and the red-light district. The hub of the area is the cosmopolitan pedestrianised garden square of Parque de Santa Catalina. Here you will find Europeans, Africans, and North Americans enjoying a drink, and indulging in the park's favourite pastime of people-watching. There are also many leisure attractions, such as a children's play area, a board-games area and so on, and on Sunday lunchtimes a musical band entertains the public.

Triana

Triana is the city's original commercial district. The area's main thoroughfare is the pedestrianised shopping street of Calle Mayor de Triana. At its northern end is the charming **Parque de San Telmo**, with a chapel and some fine dragon trees.

Just off the north end of Calle Mayor are the beautiful squares of San Francisco and Cairasco. The former houses a fine bust of Columbus, and the lovely 17th-century **Iglesia de San Francisco**. The Plaza de Cairasco is notable for the 100-year-old **Gabinete Literario** (Literary Cabinet Institute), elegantly arcaded and stuccoed, and occasionally open to the public for exhibitions (enquire at the tourist information office).

Domed kiosk–café in Parque de San Telmo

LAS PALMAS MUSEUMS
Centro Atlantico de Arte Moderno (CAAM: Atlantic Centre for Modern Art)

Although this art gallery began life as a collection of 20th century Canarian art, its focus is very much on bringing together the very different works of art created on the continents of Europe, Africa and the Americas.

Calle Los Balcones, 11. Tel: (928) 311824.
www.caam.net
Open: Tue–Sat 10am–9pm, Sun 10am–2pm. Guided tours: Tue & Fri from 7pm. Free admission.

Casa de Colón (House of Columbus)

The House of Columbus belonged to

Calle Mayor de Triana

the island's first governor, and dates originally from the 15th century. Columbus stayed here on two or three occasions en route to the New World. A museum with exhibits relating to his journeys, and a **Museum of Fine Art** are housed in the building.

Calle de Colón 1, Tel: (928) 312384.
www.cabgc.org
Open: Mon–Fri 9am–7pm, Sat & Sun 9am–3pm. Free admission. Guided tours on request.

Museo Canario (Canary Islands Museum)

This rather old-fashioned museum holds the finest collection of Guanche artefacts in the whole archipelago. Along with everyday grave finds, there is a startling display of skulls and mummies which will delight older children.

Calle Dr Vernau, 2. Tel: (928) 336800.
www.elmuseocanario.com
Open: Mon–Fri 10am–8pm, Sat–Sun 10am–2pm. Admission charge.

Museo Elder de Ciencia y Tecnología

The twin mottoes of this science museum with its 200 interactive exhibits are: 'prohibited not to learn' and 'it is forbidden not to touch'. Twenty different areas present technology with the aim of constructively entertaining children, for example with a car-welding robot and a replica space station. Some of the films shown in the giant-screen IMAX cinema are in English.

Parque de Santa Catalina. Tel: (928) 011828. www.museoelder.org
Open: Tue–Sun 10am–8pm (Fri & Sat 10pm). Admission charge; extra for cinema.

Casa Museo Pérez Galdós

The Canary Islands' favourite writer was born in this house in 1843, the last of ten children. He lived here until he moved to Madrid in 1862. It is now a museum to his memory and to encourage the study of his works. Exhibits include the writer's personal library and possessions, family furniture and various works of art. The handsome 1919 **Teatro de Pérez Galdós** opera house is close by.

Calle Cano, 6. Tel: 928 373745.
www.grancanariacultura.com/museos/pga
ldos
Open: Mon–Fri 9am–9pm, Sat
9am–6pm, Sun 10am–3pm. Guided visits
on the hour. Free admission.

A MAN FOR HIS TIMES

Benito Pérez Galdós (1843–1920) was born in Las Palmas but grew up in Madrid. He is regarded as Spain's greatest novelist after Miguel de Cervantes and on a par with his contemporaries Balzac and Dickens in describing the realities of his time. His masterpiece is *Fortunata and Jacinta* (1886–7), but his popular work in Spanish is *Episodios Nacionales*, a 46-volume fictionalisation of historical events.

A worn statue of Pérez Galdós

The Genoese sailor and explorer Christopher Columbus (Cristóbal Colón in Spanish) used the Canary Islands on several occasions as a staging post for his voyages to the New World. The records of his visits vary, and different sources argue about where he was on any one occasion. There is agreement, however, that he did stop off at Las Palmas and La Gomera in 1492.

On Gran Canaria, Columbus may have dropped anchor at Gando Bay (where the airport now is), or near the site of the present-day Puerto de la Luz in Las Palmas. From his own diary we know that just as he was passing Tenerife, Mount Teide erupted, and this was taken as an ill omen by his superstitious crew.

Columbus also stopped at La Gomera to take on water and other supplies, but another reason he may have wanted to stop here was to see the Countess of Gomera, Beatriz de Bobadilla (see p109). Columbus probably knew her from the Spanish Court – he was sailing under the flag of Ferdinand and Isabella – and there are rumours of an affair.

Columbus may have returned to La Gomera on his voyages of 1493–5 and 1498–1500. It is also thought that he visited Las Palmas on at least two occasions (either during the afore-mentioned dates, or on his last voyage of 1502–4). Other records mention

Casa de Colón, Columbus's base for expeditions to the New World

Intricate stonework on the building's façade

Maspalomas on Gran Canaria and El Hierro as stopping points.

Although in the popular imagination Columbus is remembered as one of history's undisputed achievers, his actual career was marked as much by failure as success. He was deeply religious but not humane in his treatment of the indigenous people he encountered, and he proved an incompetent governor of the colony that he founded. On one occasion he was even arrested and shipped back to Spain in chains by his patrons the king and queen. He died, poor, forgotten and resentful, still claiming he had reached Japan rather than chanced upon a new continent.

Local latter-day reactions to the great explorer are mixed. While most people on Tenerife and Gran Canaria are content to remember Columbus as more discoverer-hero than incompetent or malicious villain, Gomerans take a sterner view and side with modern critical interpretations. They no doubt remember that Columbus was involved with the slave trade, and was, at the very least, friendly with the Countess Beatriz, who tyrannised the island.

Walk: Vegueta

La Vegueta is the oldest part of Las Palmas, a nucleus of houses, mansions and churches that grew up around the first settlement built by the Castilian conquerors after 1478. It became the district where the ruling classes lived, and it still retains an aristocratic air, with splendid 17th- and 18th-century mansions decorated with coats of arms and elegantly-crafted balconies. The main sights are grouped around five attractive squares.

Allow 1 hour.

Begin in the Plaza de Santa Ana, in front of the cathedral.

1 Plaza de Santa Ana

Several interesting buildings frame the rectangular, sloping main square of La Vegueta. At the top of the square opposite the cathedral (*see p28*) is the **Casas Consistoriales** (under restoration). To the right of this is an old house with a semicircular doorway

Bronze statue in the Plaza de Santa Ana

bearing carvings of lions and castles. Further down this side of the square is the **Palacio Episcopal** (Bishop's Palace) – look through the ornate wrought iron gate to see the pretty patio. Across the square is a handsome yellow building, the **Archivo Historico Provincial**, with a plaque on the wall commemorating Pieter van der Does' attack on Las Palmas on 26 June 1599. He sacked the city but was driven off by the citizens. Adjacent is the Art Nouveau mansion of the **Colegio Oficial de Farmaceuticos**, the pharmacists' professional association.
Take the street to the left of the Casas Consistoriales.

2 Plaza del Espiritu Santo

This pleasant, triangular square has a monumental fountain in the middle and a pale turquoise building looking on to it.
Turn left across the bottom of the square and leave down the second street, Calle Doctor Chil.

3 Plaza de Santo Domingo

Go right down Calle Luis Millares to have a look at this peaceful square shaded by slender green island fig trees. Retrace your steps past the **Museo Canario** (*see p32*) and continue down Doctor Chil. There is a handsome balcony at no 22 on the left and the Café del Real on the right.

Turn left down Calle Reloj and take the first right, Calle Espiritu Santo.

4 Plaza del Pilar Nuevo

On your left is the **Museo Diocesano de Arte Sacro** (*see p28*) in the cathedral's Patio de Naranjos. Further down the street turn left into the cobbled Plaza del Pilar Nuevo and make for the green door of Casa de Colón (*see p32*). The square opens out here. Right is Calle Los Balcones, leading towards the sea. There are some handsome buildings on this street, including the **Centro Atlantico de Arte Moderno** (*see p32*), a strikingly

contemporary interior hidden behind an old façade.

From the Plaza Pilar Nuevo, follow the wall of the Casa de Colon to the right down Pasaje de Pedro de Algaba.

5 Plaza de San Antonio Abad

This is the site of origin of the first settlement. Columbus prayed in the Ermita de San Antonio Abad, although the building you see now is an 18th century reconstruction.

Take the Calle de Colón past the entrance to the museum. Cross Plazoleta de los Alamos and continue up Calle San Marcial opposite. When you get to the end turn left to reach your starting point in the Plaza de Santa Ana, or right down Calle Obispo Codina to cross the road and explore another interesting old quarter, Triana (see p31).

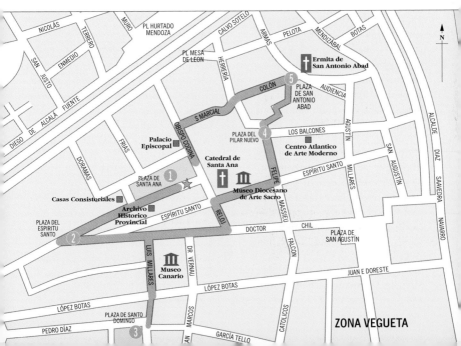

Northern Gran Canaria

If you are in search of typical Gran Canarian settlements, head north. The small towns and villages here are self-contained farming communities and rely neither on tourism nor on the wealth of Las Palmas. The coast road provides spectacular views down to the wild northwest fringes and across to Tenerife.

Arucas cathedral

Arucas

A towering, Neo-Gothic cathedral is the last thing you would expect to see in the midst of a whitewashed Canarian farming community. It was started in 1909 and completed in the late 1970s as an ostentatious sign of the town's wealth – founded in no small part on the locally produced *ron* (rum), on sale on all the islands. At night it is attractively floodlit. Near the church is a small botanic garden (the **Parque Municipal**) and a statue to the Guanche king, Doramas. Legend has it that he was slain treacherously while challenging the conquistador Pedro de Vera to single combat on Montaña de Arucas in 1481, now site of a viewpoint and restaurant. *17km west of Las Palmas.*

El Cenobio de Valerón

Although '*cenobio*' means 'convent', the theory that this honeycomb of Guanche caves set into a sheer rock face housed a community of young unmarried women has long been discounted. It is now known that the 300-odd caves, hollows and silos which were dug on various levels of the cliff using stone and bone tools, and linked to each other by steps and passages, served as a granary where barley and other crops could be kept dry and safe. Families are thought to have owned one or more of the caves which were grouped together so that they could be protected communally. Each family's property was marked using a stamp made from clay.
Cuesta de Silva, east of Santa Maria de Guía on the old road between Las Palmas and Gáldar (C 801). Open: Wed–Sun 10am–5pm. Free admission.

Gáldar

This busy, workaday town, once the capital of the island, has several points of interest. In the main square, look inside the courtyard of the Town Hall (open weekday mornings only), where the ancient dragon tree is said to be the oldest on the island. Also in the square is the Iglesia de Santiago de los Caballeros, a church dating from 1872 and containing many fine sculptures.

The Cueva Pintada (Painted Cave), at the southwest end of town, is a small Guanche cave with painted geometric figures, only discovered in 1873. It now forms the centrepiece of the Parque Arqueológico de la Cueva Pintada, together with a museum. The other

Guanche legacy nearby (in a neglected state) is an 11th-century cemetery, thought to be the last resting place of Guanche nobles.
31km west of Las Palmas.
Parque Arqueológico de la Cueva Pintada: to be open to the public shortly.

Reptilandia
This zoological park in Gáldar contains more than 500 species, ranging from scorpions, tarantulas and turtles to lizards, crocodiles, iguanas and monkeys.

Snake and other reptile feeding is on Sun at 3pm.
El Cerrillal. Tel: (928) 551269. Open: daily 11am–5.30pm.

Teror
Architecturally, this is the most typical Canarian town on the island, with beautifully preserved white houses and dozens of perfectly carved wooden balconies. It is also the religious centre of Gran Canaria, with a statue of the Virgin housed in the town's splendid 18th-century basilica. The only house open to the public is the atmospheric 17th-century **Casa de los Patronos de la Virgen del Pino**, now a museum with a beautiful patio. Shops sell traditional lace and scents made from local flora.
23km southwest of Las Palmas. Museo de la Fundación Patronos de la Virgen, Plaza Nuestra Señora del Pino. Tel: (928) 630239. Open: daily 10am–5pm. Admission charge.

Typical Canarian architecture in Teror

Jardín Botánico Canario
(Canary Islands Botanical Garden)

This luxuriant garden – the largest in Spain – was founded in 1952 by the Swede Eric Sventenius and is now maintained by the Gran Canaria island government. It follows a ravine at the base of a cliff and aims to create as near natural conditions as possible in order to study and display virtually every type of plant indigenous to the island grouping of Macaronesia (see pp42–3).

One of the treasures at the Jardín Botánico

Well-cared for by an expert team of horticulturalists, with a network of permanent paths and clear signposts, the garden is an ideal way to get to know the various ecosystems that have given rise to the Canary Islands' native flora. The garden teems with birds and butterflies and even the few weeds do not seem out of place.

La Calzada, near Tafira Alta, 7km southwest of Las Palmas. Tel: (928) 219582. Open: daily 9am–6pm. Free admission. The garden can be entered from the top of the cliff, next to the restaurant, but the main entrance is at the bottom, on the flat.

Plaza Matias Vega
The main entrance leads into this square popularly known as the Plaza de las Palmeras because it is shaded by several Canary palm trees (*Phoenix canariensis*). This is distinguishable from the date palm by its denser, more rounded, dark green foliage. Large specimens can reach 25m and have a trunk of almost a metre in diameter. On La Gomera, Canary palms are bled to make a kind of honey.

Jardín de las Islas (Islands Garden) and the Cactus Garden
Turn right from the entrance and you pass a group of dragon trees on your left and the Jardín de las Islas on your right – two lawns around which plants from Macaronesia are grouped according to their island of origin. Just beyond this is the Cactus garden with 2,000 types of moisture-hoarding plants.

Pine Woods
Continue in the same direction and you can cross the ravine by means of a wooden bridge. To the right of the next junction are stands of Canary pine trees (*Pinus canariensis*), the typical tree of many upland areas.

Laurisilva Woods
Taking the other path from the junction near the wooden bridge brings you to the delightfully named Fuente de los Sabios (Fountain of the Wise Men). A short path from here takes you through the dense dark laurisilva woods. This is the type of vegetation which used to cover much of the Canary Islands before

the arrival of the Spanish and is similar to the subtropical forest which covered much of the Mediterranean basin in the Tertiary era. Evergreen laurisilva forest needs high humidity and is confined to north facing slopes between 400 and 1,500 m of altitude where winds form 'seas of cloud'. Eighteen species of tree are present in the forest and they drip with lianas. On the forest floor where little light but much moisture reaches, mosses, ferns and lichens thrive.

This brings you to the exhibition hall. From here a stone bridge leads back to the entrance, or you can skirt round the pond and climb the zigzag path to the restaurant from which there is a view over the garden.

An overview of the Botanical Garden

Flora

There are about 2,000 different species of plants growing wild in the Canary Islands, of which more than 500 are endemic (exclusive to the islands). By comparison, the British Isles cover an area 34 times larger but have only 1,600 species, with less than 20 of them endemic. Many plants in the Canaries are only of interest to botanists, but the species mentioned below can usually be seen without ever having to leave the beaten track.

The biggest and most famous inhabitant of the islands is the dragon tree. A peculiarity of this tree is its lack of rings, which means that telling its age is very difficult. The largest and oldest tree, the Drago Milenario (at Icod de los Vinos, Tenerife), is between 500 and 3,000 years old. Guanches attributed magical properties to the tree and used its 'dragon's blood' sap (which turns red in the air) to heal wounds.

Other strange Canarian trees are the twisted and dead-looking *sabinas* (junipers) of El Hierro, while the protected laurisilva laurel forest of La Gomera is a wet, dark, spooky place to explore. By way of contrast, the tall, light, graceful Canary Pine is found on higher ground on all the western islands and Gran Canaria. The endemic tree of the dry eastern islands is the Canary date palm (which does not produce fruit), a close relative of the North African variety. Flora that do bear a harvest are the banana plant and the almond tree, both of which are imports.

The prettiest plants on the islands – bougainvillea, hibiscus, poinsettia, and the graceful *strelitzia* (bird-of-paradise flower) – have also been brought here from other countries.

The largest and most striking endemic flower is the slender red viper's bugloss or *tajinaste (Echium wildpretii)*, which grows up to 2m high in the Cañadas del Teide park. Also here (and in many other places) is the yellow or white *retama*, or Teide broom, which gives off a wonderful, pungent-sweet scent.

The most noticeable plants of the drier regions are the New World cacti, prickly pears, imported to attract cochineal bugs, and the endemic cactus-like *cardón*

An old postcard showing a dragon tree at La Laguna (below), and a more modern example from Bananera el Guanche (bottom right)
Right: succulent at Palmitos Parque

(Euphorbia canariensis). This is a candelabra spurge with tall, smooth stems (like organ pipes in appearance), very common in the south of Gran Canaria. Other succulents include several species of *senecios* and *tabaibas* – small spiky plants, resembling yucca trees, which are very tenacious, and soon colonise deserted house roofs.

Eastern Gran Canaria

It may be hard to believe that there is life beyond the soulless strip of the GC1 motorway and barren east coast, but just a few kilometres inland are wealthy villages, a sub-tropical *barranco* (ravine), a colonised crater, and the island's second city.

Vega de San Mateo

Pico de Bandama
A spiralling road leads to the top of the extinct volcano of Bandama (569m) from which there is a spectacular view over and into the crater (*see pp46–7*) and down to Las Palmas.
10km south of Las Palmas.

Barranco de Guayadeque
The spectacular ravine of Guayadeque drains almost from the centre of the island to the coast. It can be reached either from Ingenio or Agüimes. Shortly after the two roads converge there is a visitor's centre explaining the history and flora and fauna of the ravine. About three kilometres further on there is a colony of inhabited caves together with a cave-church. After another seven kilometres of splendid scenery the road comes to an end at a restaurant, but the ravine continues and a walking route leads up to the Caldera de los Marteles (1,520m).

On the road entering the ravine from the GC1 look for a small sign on the right-hand side before Agüimes centre which leads to **Cocodrilo (Crocodile) Park**, whose resident reptiles enthral children.
Guayadeque Information Centre. Open: Tue–Sat 9am–5pm, Sun 10am–6pm. Admission charge.

Cocodrilo Park. Tel: (928) 784725. Open: Sun–Fri 10am–6pm. Admission charge.

Cuatro Puertas
This has one of the most interesting aboriginal sites on the island, **the Holy Mountain of the Guanches**, dating from the palaeolithic period.
Situated between Ingenio and Telde on the C815.

Ingenio
Ingenio is a prosperous market town that also boasts a tradition of handicrafts. You can visit some of the town's *artesanías* (craft workshops) on the main road towards Telde (the C816 road). Also on this road, just outside town, is **the Museo de Piedras y Artesanía Canaria** (Museum of Rocks and Canarian handicrafts). It is a strange mix of old-fashioned geological exhibits, embroidery, and gaudy religious displays.
Ingenio is 12km south of Telde.
Museum open: Mon–Sat 8am–6.30pm. Free admission.

Telde
Gran Canaria's second city owes its wealth to its 16th-century sugarcane trade, and grand mansions of this

period can be found in the San Juan district to the north of the town. In the same quarter is the jewel of the city – the richly decorated 15th-century **Iglesia de San Juan de Bautista** (Church of St John the Baptist). It has a

splendidly carved early 16th-century Flemish altarpiece and, from the same period, an intriguing life-size figure of Christ, made in Mexico from corn husks and weighing just 5kg.

The centre of Telde is now a one-way street system with many interesting small shops, and a market on Saturday mornings.
14km south of Las Palmas.

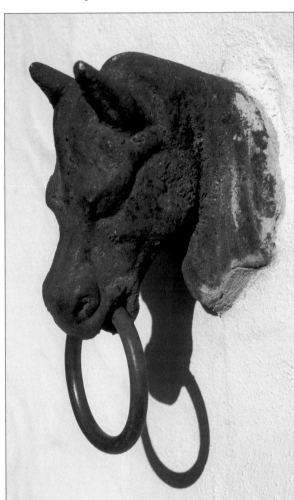

Local handiwork

Vecindario

This typically Spanish town is gradually transforming itself into a place for tourists to visit. It has a large new commercial centre, a hotel and a cinema that shows up-to-date films in English some afternoons. Most people find a Wednesday morning browsing around the market, followed by lunch in one of the many cafés or restaurants, and then a walk around the commercial centre, make a good day out.
15km north of Playa del Inglés on the C812.

Walk: Caldera de Bandama

The Caldera de Bandama is said to be the most perfectly formed volcanic crater in the Canary Islands. Each year, thousands of coach trippers gaze down into the *caldera* from the *mirador* (viewpoint) above – yet very few tourists (or even locals) actually venture down to the valley floor. It's a short but very steep trek to this tiny Shangri-la. Anyone who is moderately fit can do the walk. If it's a nice day, take a drink and picnic.

Allow 1¹/₂ hours.

Mirador at the Caldera de Bandama

FRAGILE WORLD

The Caldera de Bandama is of great interest. Guanche caves are located on the sheer, higher levels, though only the more daring try to explore them. Botanists also come down into the valley to conduct plant trials in this unique environment. Unfortunately, tourist coaches are causing the side of the crater to slip away (there are plans to re-route heavy vehicles). Walkers should also be sensitive to the environment, and stay on the given paths in order to prevent damage to plant-life and the environment.

Follow the roadsigns for the Campo de Golf, and park as close to the Hotel de Golf as possible.

The views on both sides of the road are magnificent. To the *caldera* side you can see the whole of the 1,000m-diameter crater opening before you; to the golf club side you can see far beyond the club house and hotel, with carpets of green leading to the distant hills.

Walk back along the road for half a kilometre until you come to the Restaurant Los Geranios. Go down the short road between the restaurant and bus stop and you will come to the steps leading down into the caldera.

After 20 or so large steps the path becomes a narrow dirt track. Don't worry about getting lost – there's just one way, and that's down, 200m to the valley floor. It only takes 15 minutes to make the steep descent but it will take you much longer to get back up. Towards the bottom of the track you will see, down to the left, the farm where an elderly farmer still lives and works. This path is his only contact with the outside world.

Once on the valley floor, follow the path leading between the drystone walls to the tall, shady eucalyptus trees. In winter, the valley floor is a splendid sight, carpeted with bright yellow flowering trefoils, divided neatly by drystone walls and decorated by tall palms and fruit-laden orange trees. The whole scene, complete with its low rustic farmhouses and grazing goats, is more akin to a rather exotic English meadow than an arid Canarian island.

This is effectively the centre of the caldera. Retrace your route to the starting point.

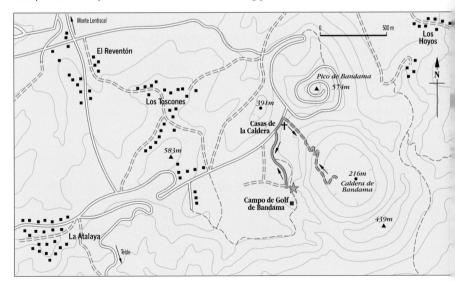

Central Gran Canaria

The heart of the island was once a sacred point for the Guanches, and their totem rocks, Nublo and Bentaiga, still dominate an epic mountain landscape. Breathtaking *miradores* (viewpoints) are the hallmark of this area, offering magnificent views of the island and beyond.

Roque Bentaiga

Artenara

At an altitude of 1,200m, this peaceful whitewashed settlement, clinging to the mountainside, is certainly the highest, and arguably the most spectacular village on the island. The views across the ravine, either from the pretty terrace of the Méson de Silla restaurant, or from the square next to the church, are legendary. Not so well known, however, is the village's small cave-church (up the hill, opposite the main church).
18km northwest of Cruz de Tejeda.

Cruz de Tejeda

On a clear day you can see Mount Teide on Tenerife from this 1,450m mountain pass and crossroads but on most days you can still see two other landmarks closer to hand, the **Roque Bentaiga** and the **Roque Nublo**. For many people the crossroads is a place to eat, drink or shop for souvenirs. The island's *parador* restaurant faces the hotel-restaurant complex of El Refugio across the road, between them the *cruz* itself – a finely carved stone cross. Heading south from here, the landscapes are in striking contrast to the green and wooded slopes to the north, with great crags and fingers of rock rising up out of dry terrain.

43km southwest of Las Palmas, 45km north of Maspalomas.

Los Pinos de Gáldar

The *mirador* of 'the pines of Gáldar' is a vantage point unlike many in the mountainous interior. Here, the view stumbles over the edge of a crater, slides down verdant pine-covered hillsides, and descends for over 40km, taking in the whole of the north coast.
9km north of Cruz de Tejeda.

Pico de las Nieves

The 'Peak of the Snows' is the geographic centre and highest point of Gran Canaria at 1,949m above sea level. Cloud permitting, the views of the island's mountainous interior are quite stunning from here.
8km southeast of Cruz de Tejeda.

Pinar de Tamadaba

The *pinar* (pine forest) of Tamadaba is a beautiful area of tall, slender pines to the northwest of Artenara. A narrow circular road snakes up to around 1,400m and, if the weather is clear, it will reward you with a priceless view of Mount Teide, seemingly floating above the clouds.
25km northwest of Cruz de Tejeda.

Roque Bentaiga/Cueva del Rey

Roque Bentaiga was a sacred spot to the Guanches, and goats were once sacrificed on the simple altar which still stands here. It is possible to walk up to the summit (1,404m), but you must be very sure-footed and have a head for heights. Along the same track (past the Bentaiga turning) is the **Cueva del Rey** (King's Cave). Stop your car when a tall crag looms to your left, and the road dives downhill to your right. Walk round the mountainside to your left and the Cueva del Rey, once the royal abode, is high above in the honeycombed rock. The views from here, across to Artenara, are truly fit for a king. It is possible to climb up to the caves, but be careful.

As if to confirm the Guanches' mystic views, from certain angles, the rock next to Bentaiga takes on the appearance of a robed holy man – hence its name, Roque El Fraile ('The Monk').
On the C811 between Cruz de Tejeda and Ayacata (44km from Las Palmas).

Roque Nublo (Cloud Rock)

It is claimed that this landmark pinnacle, pointing 1,803m into the Canarian sky, is the world's highest basalt monolith. Like Roque Bentaiga, this, too, was once a holy site. If you want to walk to the rock, it's just over 6km from the nearest accessible approach point of La Culata.
La Culata is 1km north of Ayacata.

Stone cross at Cruz de Tejeda

Fataga and Las Tirajanas

Heading inland from Maspalomas the GC520 road climbs into a nature reserve, twists around a ridge and drops down into the scenic Barranco de Fataga. This deep ravine, lush in places, has been dubbed the 'Valley of a Thousand Palm trees'. It leads up to the village of Fataga itself, beyond which, contained within a rugged *caldera*, are the towns of San Bartolomé and Santa Lucia. This corner of the island contains few attractions or particular points of interest but it is worth visiting for its natural beauty, with its stark and dramatic hillsides, surprisingly densely populated, punctuated by lush and fertile corners of cultivation.

The land around Fataga is very fertile

Degollada de las Yeguas

This viewpoint on a bend of the road up from Maspalomas is the best place to take in the scenery of the Barranco de Fataga and the surrounding hills which are dotted with cactuses, shrubs and succulents. The steep slopes are home to some rare plants.

Barranco de Fataga

The settlement of Fataga (population just over 319) itself is no more than a handful of whitewashed houses around a small archetypal church, but it is a thriving centre that serves the surrounding countryside with its shops, bar, hotel and restaurant. It is also a winemaking centre and the *bodega* can be visited if you want an introduction to Gran Canaria's wine industry. Down the ravine towards Maspalomas is Arteara, a hamlet of 40 inhabitants amid a cluster of palm trees. Two camel farms here offer safaris to visitors.

Fataga is 20km north of Maspalomas Faro.
Bodega Tabaibilla. Tel: (928) 763906.
Open: Mon–Sat 9am–5pm, Sun 9am–12 midday.
La Baranda Camel Safari Park.
Tel: (928) 798680.
Manolo's Camel Safari.
Tel: (928) 798686.

San Bartolomé de Tirajana

High up in the Caldera de Tirajana is the region's main town. Most of the time it is a quiet place of not much interest but on Sunday mornings it holds a lively market.

From the spa hotel of Las Tirajanas (*see p167*), which stands above the road down to Fataga, you can get a majestic overview of the whole region, from the white dots of houses climbing the slopes as high as possible to a glimpse of the sea at Maspalomas Faro.
28 km north of Maspalomas Faro.

Santa Lucía de Tirajana

From San Bartolomé the road snakes around, down and across the Barranco de Tirajana to this, the most attractive of the three towns in the area, sited on the eastern side of the *caldera* among almond trees, palms, prickly pears and eucalyptus trees. The church, with its large white Moorish-looking dome, is a landmark for miles around. Next to it is a well-tended public park. The only other points of interest are the privately-owned Museo Castillo de la Fortaleza, a folk and archaeology museum housed in a mock-fortress, and, some way out of town, another fortress in name only, the rock formation of Fortaleza de Ansite.
31km north of Maspalomas.
Church open: Mon–Sat 10am–5pm, Sun noon–4pm. Admission charge. Museum. Tel: (928) 798310. Open: daily 10am–6.30pm. Admission charge.

Dramatic scenery near Fataga

Maspalomas

As surely as nature has created the rugged interior of Gran Canaria, so developers have created the streamlined holiday world of Maspalomas, officially the shoreline of the municipality of San Bartolomé de Tirajana (*see p50*), which is marketed under the brand of 'Costa Canaria'. The 17 kilometre sprawl of apartment blocks, hotels, shops and restaurants mercifully extends hardly any distance in land and is relieved by some of the island's best beaches, a Sahara-like nature reserve and the odd example of tasteful architecture.

Maspalomas lighthouse

This cosmopolitan leisure complex is as popular with gays as it is with families and there seems to be space for everyone to do their own thing. Although the buildings merge together the resort is made up of three basic units: the original nucleus of Maspalomas, Playa del Inglés and San Agustín.

Maspalomas is 58km south of Las Palmas. Tourist office: next to the entrance of Centro Comercial Yumbo, Avenida de Estados Unidos Playa del Inglés. Tel: (928) 762591.

Maspalomas (Faro)

Until the early 1960s Maspalomas was simply an oasis of palm trees by some sand dunes, underneath a 65-metre lighthouse (the Faro) which was built in 1886. The lighthouse still stands proud and somehow the saltwater lagoon of La Charca has managed to survive as a resting place for birds migrating between Africa and Europe. But what characterises Maspalomas today are luxury hotels and a long attractive beach extending west, more intimate than the featureless stretches to the east. The paseo de Meloneras runs alongside it towards the neighbouring resort of Pasito Blanco. Behind the dunes is a championship golf course (*see p151*) with self-catering bungalows around it. A conference centre (*see p173*) draws in a business clientele.

The resort's biggest man-made attraction is Holiday World, the first amusement park in the Canaries. All the usual favourites are here: a landmark ferris wheel, swingboats, bumper cars (and boats), phantom jets, and so on. *Holiday World Avenida Touroperador. Tel: (928) 730498. Open: daily 6pm–midnight. Admission charge (covers all rides).*

Dunas de Maspalomas

Spectacular desert-like dunes are the natural trademark of Maspalomas. Despite their Saharan appearance they were not blown in from Africa, nor were they shipped here as a tourist attraction (as was Las Teresitas beach on Tenerife). They are a product of sea and wind forces peculiar to this area. The dunes have always been protected from development, but anybody is free to walk across them. Don't be surprised if you are confronted by nudists or a tourist camel train; both use the dunes frequently. One of the best views of the dunes is at sunset from the terrace of the Hotel Riu Palace in Playa del Inglés.

San Agustín

Although the very first hotel on the Costa Canaria was built here in the early 1960s, San Agustín has remained the most restrained of the three parts of Maspalomas and is largely given over to low-rise apartments with attractive gardens. It draws an older clientele who don't seem to mind that their beach is the darkest coloured of the three, although it does have the advantage of being screened by a low cliff.
9km east of Maspalomas Faro.

Playa del Inglés

The name of this resort-within-a-resort, 'Beach of the English', is somewhat misleading, as you will find many different north European nationalities here. It was created on barren land during the 1960s, and has become a super-compressed labyrinth of hotels, apartments, cheap restaurants, bars and ugly *centros commerciales* (shopping centres). The only possible point of sightseeing interest is the intriguing Ecumenical Church, which resembles a portion of the Sydney Opera House. Behind Playa del Inglés is the residential area of San Fernando.

The spectacular dunes at Maspalomas

MASPALOMAS ENVIRONS

Although the resort of Maspalomas looks towards the beach for its main appeal, and many visitors are content to do very little but lie in the sunshine, there are a number of attractions in the arid hinterland which are particularly geared up towards families. All of them are reachable by bus from the resort.

Aqualand Maspalomas

Gran Canaria's biggest water park can make a busy day out for kids with its 33 water slides organised into 13 themes, with fearsome names such as Kamikaze and Adrenalina, and the spiralling Anaconda. The star attraction is the dizzying Tornado with its blue-and-yellow checkered bowls. There are a few more relaxing rides, such as the Congo river, and also activities suitable for younger children.

On the road to Palmitos Park, km 3. Tel: (928) 140525. Open: daily 10am–6pm. Admission charge.

Palmitos Park

Arguably the most popular family attraction on Gran Canaria, this ornithological theme park is beautifully set in a canyon and boasts 150 species of bird, 1,000 palm trees and 15,000 other, mainly subtropical, plants. There are regular displays of cockatoos and parrots, eagles, falcons, owls and other birds of prey and exotic birds (marabous, ibises, Kookaburrahs). But what may appeal most are the number of birds at liberty or, as with the flamingoes and ibises, at semi-liberty in the 'interactive enclosure'. Other birds to see include toucans, hummingbirds, hornbills, cranes and macaws.

Even if you are not a bird fan, there are plenty of other animals in the park: a pair of gibbons, Europe's biggest butterfly house and an aquarium with a stingray pool. Alternative attractions are the gardens, including a cacti garden and an orchid house.

Barranco de los Palmitos, 10km north of Maspalomas (bus no 45). Tel: (928) 140276. Open: daily 10am–6pm. Admission charge.
Bird Displays (commentaries in English, Spanish and German):
Parrots: 10.30am, 2.30pm, 3.30pm & 4.30pm
Birds of Prey: 12.30 & 2.30pm
Exotic Birds: 1.30 & 3.30pm

Mundo Aborigen

An inhabitant of Palmitos Park

Mundo Aborigen

This open-air museum in the mountains behind Maspalomas is a historical theme park recreating the way the Guanches lived before the Spanish conquest of the Canary Islands. A marked trail leads the visitor past scenes of everyday life peopled by life-size figures – a butcher chopping up a carcass, a doctor engaged in surgery, a farmer sowing his crops, the execution of a criminal and so on. Recorded sound effects add extra reality. Shows and demonstrations are also staged to bring the Guanche world more alive.

Parque Natural de Ayagaures 6km from Playa del Inglés on the road to Fataga and San Bartolomé de Tirajana. Bus no 18 from San Fernando in Maspalomas. Tel: (928) 172295. Open: daily 9am–6pm. Admission charge.

Sioux City

You can forget you are in Spain for a few hours in this 'paella-Western' theme park set against the backdrop of a canyon reminiscent of genuine Wild West scenery. Here stuntmen stage bank hold-ups, shoot-outs, lassoings and lynchings, and wily Mexican hombres perform knife-throwing acts. More relaxing are the dance routines of the guys and gals in the saloon. On Friday nights there is a barbecue dinner with live country music.

Cañon del Aguila, 3km north of San Agustín. Bus number 29 from Playa del Inglés and Faro. Tel: (928) 762573. Open: Tue–Sun 10am–5pm. Shows. Admission charge.

Southern Resorts

Away from the large Maspalomas conurbation, Gran Canaria's south coast has a range of holiday resorts to choose from. In places, row upon row of white boxes obscure the hillsides above the sea and the only way of getting away from it all can be to take to the sea. Puerto de Mogán, however, demonstrates how tourism can be combined with sensitivity to the surroundings and beyond it there is still some spectacular natural scenery to enjoy.

Puerto de Mogán

Arguineguín

Arguineguín, not to be confused with the adjacent La Playa de Arguineguín/Patalavaca tourist development, is the only genuine fishing village on this part of the coast. Market day, Tuesday, is the best time to visit; there is also a daily fish auction at the port.
12km west of Maspalomas.

Pasito Blanco

This new marina development with berthing room for up to 500 pleasure craft occupies a pretty cove. Big-game fishing boats can be hired, and it is always interesting to see the catches being proudly exhibited late in the afternoon.
6km west of Maspalomas Faro.

Playa de Amodores

This is a beautiful, new, man-made beach within a sheltered bay with shower and toilet facilities. There are cafés and restaurants nearby. Get there by bus or car.
5km west of Puerto Rico.

Puerto Rico

With its wonderful location in a crescent-shaped bay and stretches of golden sand, it is no wonder that Puerto Rico is popular. However, like many popular resorts it can get overcrowded.

The other appeal of Puerto Rico lies in its watersports and fishing facilities. It has the best pleasure harbour on the island, and both its sailing school and its fishing charters enjoy international fame.
18km west of Maspalomas.

Puerto de Mogán

Puerto de Mogán is a good example of sympathetic Canarian holiday development. The old fishing harbour has been expanded to a traffic-free 'village' of local-style houses, painted white with a pastel trim, each with a wrought-iron balcony and pretty window boxes or garden. The houses cluster around a new pleasure marina, joined coherently by arches and bridges. Shops and restaurants are well-kept.

The original fishing fleet is still here and gives a genuine local touch to the marina. There is a small black beach next to the port, but most visitors prefer to make the short boat trip to the golden sands of Puerto Rico.
32km west of Maspalomas.

Colourful bougainvillea in Puerto de Mogán

PUTTING TO SEA

Whether you want to go dolphin watching, deep sea fishing or merely laze about on a boat for an hour or two, you'll almost certainly find a boat to suit your taste in Puerto Rico and Puerto Mogán. Some of the options include:

Lineas Salmon Tel: (649) 919383. Regular glass-bottom boat service between Arguineguín, Puerto Rico, and Puerto de Mogán.

Bouche-en-coeur Tel: (928) 562503 Sailing boat carrying a maximum of 18 passengers. If you're lucky you might see dolphin and flying fish.

Windjammer San Miguel Tel: (928) 760076. Fully-rigged sailing ship which departs daily from Puerto Rico at 10.30am.

Cruceros Timanfaya Tel: (928) 268280. Imitation pirate ship which departs from Puerto Rico at 11am and sails as far as the Bahia de Mogán.

Western Gran Canaria

The steep terrain of Gran Canaria's west coast means that this area is sparsely populated and relatively untouched by tourism. If there are few sights worth seeing between Agaete in the northwest and Puerto de Mogán on the southwest coast, then at least it means you are more likely to escape the crowds as you make your way along the tortuous curves of the C810 road.

The coast near Dedo de Dios

Agaete

This picturesque small town lies in a particularly fertile belt, with exotic fruits among its many crops. It is the only place in Europe where coffee is grown, although only as a secondary crop on field borders. The town's showpiece is the Huerto de las Flores (Garden of the Flowers), a garden of tropical and subtropical plants. In the town square old men doze on park benches in front of the large, red-domed church. La Virgen de las Nieves is well worth a visit, as is the nearby archaeological excavation site of Malpais.

The port of Agaete, Puerto de las Nieves, is where the Fred Olsen ferry to Tenerife is based. It is a windswept spot with a small promenade overlooking wild cliff scenery and a black pebble beach. The famous rock, Dedo de Dios (Finger of God), is seen here.
41km west of Las Palmas. Huerto de las Flores is a small enclosed park in the centre of the village. Open: dawn to dusk. Free admission.

Cactualdea Park

As the name suggests, the stars of this garden just to the north of San Nicolas are cacti which flourish in the climate of western Gran Canaria. Around 1,200 different species belonging to 900 families are cultivated and many of them are on sale in the greenhouses. Cactualdea is a family day out with animals to see (camels, goats, ostriches and peacocks) and a variety of events staged in an amphitheatre. These include *salto del pastor* (a game employing a shepherd's staff), *juego de palo* (a game played by two opponents wielding sticks) and Canary Islands' wrestling, *lucha canaria.* There is a restaurant on site, a craft market and a wine cellar with 250 types of wine, many of which can be tasted.
Calle Tocodoman, La Aldea de San Nicolás. Tel: (928) 891228. www.canary-guide.com/gc/cactualdea Open: daily 10am–6pm. Admission charge.

Mogán

This small, pretty, quiet hill-village is a breath of fresh air after the crowded coastal strip – its gardens and countryside abound with exotic tropical fruits and flowers. For a picnic, take the minor C811 road 10km north to the beautifully situated Embalse de Cueva de las Niñas ('The Little Girls' Cave Reservoir') which has barbecue facilities.

Another point of outstanding natural beauty, Los Azulejos, lies 11km north of Mogán on the road to San Nicolás.
9km north of Puerto de Mogán.

San Nicolás de Tolentino

San Nicolás is a major agricultural centre in a fertile valley. Its great silvery netted greenhouse-like fields are landmarks which can be seen as far away as the centre of the island. The straggling town itself is of no great interest, but its port (known as Puerto de la Aldea) is worth a visit for its fish restaurants and the views from its attractive black pebble beach. San Nicolás is also the gateway to the most spectacular drive on the island (*see p60*).
64km northwest of Maspalomas.

Whitewashed church at Agaete

Drive: Route of the Reservoirs

GRAN CANARIA

San Nicolás
de Tolentino

Pico de
las Nieves

Maspalomas

This excursion through the wild interior of the island is as spectacular a route as any on the archipelago, climbing from an altitude of 64m to 1,200m. This is a favourite route for organised jeep safaris, but although the road is rough in parts, a four-wheel drive vehicle is not necessary. However, the narrow, winding roads are often unprotected from steep drops, so care and confidence are needed. Don't attempt it in an ordinary car if the weather is poor. The route is just 29km long, but driving conditions are slow. *Allow 2 hours.*

Start from the centre of San Nicolás de Tolentino. Follow the small yellow directional arrow to Artenara (left, right, and left again).

Spring is a good time to catch the blossom

1 San Nicolás

The route starts on narrow tracks set amid tall fields of tomatoes and papayas and ramshackle smallholdings. Leaving the fields, the road climbs sharply, following the line of the Barranco de la Aldea, and is very rough. After around 7km, it flattens out and becomes smoother. There is a bar and the Embalse (Reservoir) del Caidero to your right.

By now the scenery is breathtaking, with peak upon peak rising sharply as far as the eye can see. The valley floor is lush around the reservoirs, but the mountains are stark in greys, and shades of red and pink.

A little further on to the right, the clear blue waters of the Presa de Siberio come into view (a *presa* is a small reservoir).

The road climbs up to a mirador (16km past San Nicolás), where there is the shell of a small windmill, minus its sails, that now resembles a sentry box. From here there are wonderful views down to the Embalse de Parralillo and the Presa de Siberio.

2 Embalse de Parralillo (Parralillo Reservoir)

This is the most striking of all the reservoirs. If the light is right it will take on a deep, emerald green hue, but in any shade of blue or green it is a fine sight. Across to the east you can see quite clearly the Guanches' sacred rocks of Bentaiga (large and square), and behind it, to the right, Nublo, a smaller, though higher pinnacle (*see p49*).

The road climbs slowly up towards the centre of the island, approaching Roque Bentaiga. After 22km the route reaches the village of Acusa.

3 Acusa

The Route of the Reservoirs ends in green fields near Acusa, at the Church of La Candelaria.

Way down below, to the left, is the last of the reservoirs, the Presa de la Candelaria. (If you would like to see some cave dwellings, follow the sign to Acusa.)

Unless you are visiting the caves, keep on the road left to Artenara. Turn right at the Cruz de Acusa crossroads at 26km, and after a further 3km you will come to Artenara.

4 Artenara

To end the trip on a high note enjoy the magnificent views from the church square, or you could stop for a typically Canarian snack at the Méson de la Silla restaurant (on the road directly above the approach road to the village), where the view is just as spectacular, and even more beautifully framed.

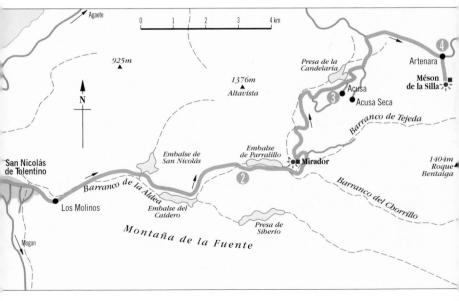

All distant isles attract myths and legends, and the hoariest island legend of all – Atlantis – is often connected with the Canaries. Plato described Atlantis as lying to the west of Gibraltar. Some 10,000 years before his time, so Plato wrote, it had been sent to the bottom of the ocean by earthquakes and tidal waves, until only seven mountain tops remained above the waters. Could this be the Canaries? Atlantis, a happy and wealthy land, also sounds rather like the Fortunate Islands, as the Canaries were described in antiquity – a land of plenty, of eternal springtime, with 'fertile soil and crops and fruit without working'.

Unfortunately for the romantics, this story does not match current theories suggesting that volcanoes created rather than destroyed the land. Plato's timescale was also inaccurate, as even the youngest islands are some two million years old.

And what should we make of the 'eighth Canary Island' – San Borondón? The island was named after St Brendan (or Brandan), a sixth-century Irish monk who sailed for seven years in search of the island where the saints were reincarnated. According to 16th-century Portuguese navigators, San Borondón lay 200–300 sea miles northwest of La Palma. By Canarian standards it was huge: 422km from north to south, and 149km from east to west. This island also had seven cities.

The legend continues that after seven years on the island, Brendan and his monks were told to leave by an angel. After yet another seven years, just as he was despairing of sighting land, an island (perhaps the same island) appeared. But immediately after the

Insulæ Fortu

monks had celebrated mass, the land rumbled; they beat a hasty retreat back to their boat, and the island sank.

Apparently, when the weather conditions are right, you can look out northwest from La Palma, and see the high mountain peaks of San Borondón –

but don't book your next holiday there just yet!

Picturesque maps illustrating the coming of Christianity to the archipelago date back to the 6th century. Evidence indicates that the islands were known to the ancient Greeks and Romans who called them Happy Islands, Garden of the Hesperides, Atlantida

Tenerife

Tenerife is the largest of the Canary Islands, and in Mount Teide boasts the highest point in all Spanish territory. Consequently, the weather contrasts here are greater than on any other island. In winter, the wind may whistle and snow may drift around Mount Teide, while just 40km to the south, sunbathers bronze themselves on the beach.

The south of the island is hot, dry, and arid, with little of sightseeing interest. Its resorts are the brash new face of Tenerife. For history, culture, and scenery you have to go to the north to the fine old colonial towns of La Laguna, La Orotava, and the capital, Santa Cruz. Even Puerto de la Cruz, where tourism on Tenerife was born around a century ago, still retains much of its old character, despite its increasing number of high-rise hotels.

The north is green and lush, which, of course, means rain. Rainfall is short, sharp and only occasional in summer, but in winter it's almost guaranteed to affect a few days of a two-week stay.

Teide rises above everything on Tenerife. The volcanic scenery of its national park is out of this world, but there are plenty of other competing attractions on the island. Zoos, gardens, banana plantations, and museums mean no one need ever be at a loose end here.

Surprisingly, the only thing that Tenerife is short on is good beaches. Only the golden strip of Playa de las Teresitas (near Santa Cruz) is worth a postcard home. However, with alternatives such as the Lido at Puerto de la Cruz and Aguapark Octopus at Playa de las Américas, few people seem to mind.

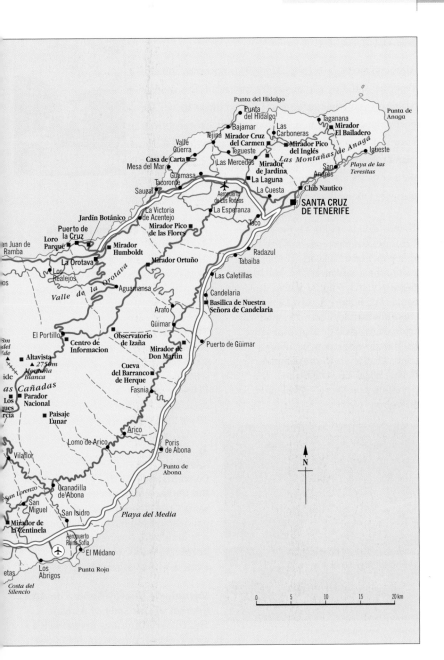

Santa Cruz

Although Santa Cruz (pop. 220,000) is now the capital of Tenerife, and the administrative centre of the western islands, it was a late developer. It began life as merely the port adjunct of the more important San Cristobal de la Laguna, but its more rapid commercial growth led to the island's institutions being moved here in 1723. Nowadays the two cities are merging together and a hyper-modern tramway linking the two will cement the conurbation.

Covered market, Santa Cruz

To most holiday visitors, however, Santa Cruz means a morning's 'tax-free' shopping in the Calle del Castillo, and a visit to the town's most colourful bazaar, the Mercado de Nuestra Señora de África. Santa Cruz is more than just a place to shop, however, it's a busy city gradually rejuvenating itself through innovative seafront developments, including a concert hall and a leisure complex.
Tourist office: Plaza de España. Tel: (922) 531107. Open: Mon–Fri 8am–6pm, Sat 9am–1pm.

Santa Cruz is a working port

Auditorio de Tenerife (Tenerife Auditorium)
This striking building by architect Santiago Calatrava is rapidly becoming the symbol of the modern city. It took almost 30 years to build from initial conception to opening its doors in 2003. The distinctive crescent-shaped canopy arches to over 50m high.
*Cruz Verde 21–23. Tel: (922) 270611. www.auditoriodetenerife.com
Open for performances only. Ticket office open: Mon–Fri 10am–2pm & 5–7pm, Sat 10am–2pm. Ticket sales: Tel: (902) 317327.*

Iglesia de Nuestra Señora de la Concepción (Church of Our Lady of the Immaculate Conception)
Santa Cruz's most important historical building was founded in 1502 but rebuilt in 1652. It contains a number of interesting works of art.
Plaza de la Iglesia. Tel: (922) 243847.

Mercado de Nuestra Señora de África (Market of Our Lady of Africa)
This colourful, bustling market sells a wide range of fruits, vegetables, flowers,

fish, and meats. On Sundays, a *rastro* (flea market) is held next to the halls. *Calle San Sebastián. Tel: (922) 214743. Open: Mon–Sat 9am–1pm.*

Calle Fuente Morales. Tel: (922) 535816. www.museosdetenerife.org Open: Tue–Sun 9am–7pm. Admission charge.

Museo de la Naturaleza y el Hombre (Museum of Man and Nature)

Located in the old Civil Hospital, the centre houses the former Archaeological Museum and the Museum of Natural Sciences. Themes include 'The Canary Islands Through Time', and 'Biological Anthropology'.

Museo Militar de Canarias (Canary Islands Military Museum)

The Almeida fort that now houses the military museum was built as a consequence of Nelson's failed attack on Santa Cruz in 1797, which showed that the port was vulnerable to a beach landing to the north. From here gun

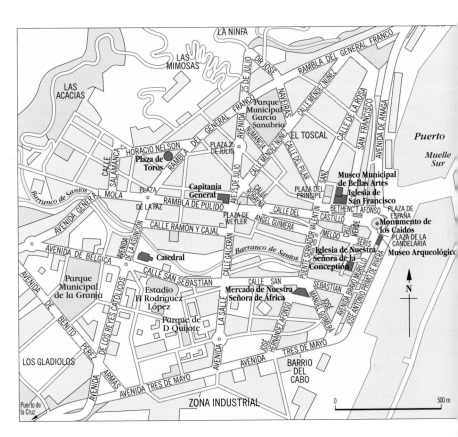

batteries were to train their sights out to sea against possible pirate attacks from the English and French. Unfortunately, the castle was only finished in 1884 by which time advances in warfare had made its cannons good for nothing but firing 21-gun military salutes. The most interesting part of the exhibition is that which deals with Nelson's attack and the prized exhibit is a cannon nicknamed *El Tigre* (the Tiger), said to be the one that fired the grapeshot at the rear admiral.

THE ENGLISH REPELLED

In July 1797, Rear Admiral Horatio Nelson, fresh from victory at the Battle of Cape St Vincent, was ordered to attack Santa Cruz de Tenerife in order to take possession of a treasure-laden Spanish galleon that was supposed to be moored there. A first assault on the town failed. Nelson led a second landing, this time at night, but the element of surprise had been lost and the Spanish garrison reinforced. Nelson was hit by grapeshot which shattered his right arm above the elbow. A surgeon on board his flagship, *HMS Theseus*, amputated the arm in the fashion of the day, without anaesthetic, using a knife and saw. The attack was repelled at the cost of 153 English dead or wounded, but the commander general of the Canary Islands, Don Antonio Gutierrez, was magnanimous in his victory: he had the English wounded transported safely back to their ships and invited the officers to dine with him that evening.

House near Plaza de la Iglesia

San Isidro 2. Tel: (922) 271658 Open: Tue–Sun, 10am–2pm. Admission charge.

Museo Municipal de Bellas Artes (Municipal Museum of Fine Arts)

The pride of this museum is its fine collection of works by Flemish and Spanish masters, including Ribera, Brueghel, Van Loo, and Jordaens.
Calle José Murphy. Tel: (922) 244358. Open: Mon–Fri 10am–1.30pm, 2.30–7pm (winter), 10am–7.30pm (summer). Free admission.

Parque Marítimo César Manrique (César Manrique Maritime Park)

A group of swimming pools and sports facilities complemented by other amenities makes up this leisure complex designed by the celebrated Lanzarote artist César Manrique but only completed after his death. As with all his work, he intended it to harmonise with its natural surroundings. A Palmetum – a specialist palm tree collection – is being added to the park, with a museum and shade house.

Avda. Constitución, 5. Tel: (922) 202995. www.indigocio.com
Open: 10am–6pm. Admission charge.

Parque Municipal García Sanabria (García Sanabria Municipal Park)

This is a beautifully laid out park with exotic trees and shrubs, fountains and statuary, a floral clock, and a small animal compound.

En route to the park are two plazas – Plaza del General Weyler, and Plaza 25 de Julio with ceramic benches decorated with museum-piece 1920s tiles.

Rambla del General Franco–Calle Mendez Nuñez.

Plaza de España

The drab, towering cross which stands in this square is a monument to the dead of the Spanish Civil War fought 1936–9. Next to it is another depressing example of Fascist architecture, the huge *Cabildo Insular* (island government offices).

Plaza de la Candelaria

The centre of this square is dominated by a statue illustrating El Triunfo de la Candelaria (Triumph of the Virgin of Candelaria, *see p100*) by the renowned Italian sculptor Antonio Canova (1757–1822). The figures on guard at the corner represent Guanche chieftains (*see pp14–15*).

Look into the bank at No. 9 on the Plaza. This was formerly the Palacio de Carta, built in 1742, and contains a perfect example of a Canarian patio.

Calle del Castillo, leading off from here, is the town's main shopping street.

Government buildings on Plaza de España

The Anaga Mountains

Despite its great beauty, the panoramic, green-cloaked Anaga Mountains region is still relatively unexplored, and small villages, cut off from the main roads, form a genuinely 'hidden Tenerife'. It is an excellent area for walking, and this is the only way to do it justice. However, it is also an easy area to tour by car, with several fine *miradores* guaranteeing a memorable trip.

View from Mirador de Jardina

Bajamar

Bajamar is one of the oldest tourist resorts on the island, popular with German visitors. Like its fellow veteran, Puerto de la Cruz, it has only a small, black beach to offer its guests, and so the pools by the promenade are popularly used for swimming.

Punta del Hidalgo, 3km to the north, is its newer sister resort. Many of the hotels here enjoy excellent cliff-top positions. The sunset views from here are said to be the best on Tenerife.
Bajamar is 30km northeast of Puerto de la Cruz.

Bosque de las Mercedes

This is a primeval laurel forest, of the type that can be found on La Gomera (*see pp106–7*). This sort of vegetation is now quite rare and much prized by botanists and ecologists. It stretches from north of the village of Las Mercedes to the higher ground of the mountains.
Las Mercedes is 4km north of La Laguna.

Casa de Carta

The beautiful 18th-century Canarian house of the Carta family houses the islands' finest ethnographic collection.

The house itself is a superlative example of Canarian architecture with an equally outstanding collection of porticoes, patios, and richly carved woodwork. Its most colourful exhibits are traditional Canarian costumes, which range from the 18th century to the present day. You can see how these were made in the weaving and needlework rooms.

Other displays include reconstructions of various rooms, and a ceramics collection.
Tacoronte–Valle de Guerra road, 25km northeast of Puerto de la Cruz.
Tel: (922) 546308. Open: Tues–Sun 9am–7pm. Admission charge.

MIRADORES (VIEWPOINTS)

Cruz del Carmen

Fine views to the mountains (north) and to La Laguna and Teide (south) can be enjoyed from this elevation of 920m. An early 17th-century chapel here holds the much-venerated figure of Nuestra Señora de las Mercedes.
8km northeast of La Laguna.

De Jardina

This is the closest mirador to La Laguna, and has a splendid view into the fertile 'garden' area which makes up the city hinterland, and beyond to the east coast. *7km northeast of La Laguna.*

El Bailadero

This spectacular viewpoint, perched on a knife-edge of rock, gives a 360-degree view. The town straggling down to the north coast directly below is Taganana. *19km northeast of La Laguna.*

Pico del Inglés

One explanation for this curious name ('Peak of the English') is that, in the days of Raleigh and Hawkins, English spies sent signals from here to their marauding ships whenever a Spanish galleon was sighted. It is the highest (992m) and the best of all the Anaga vantage points, offering a panorama of the mountains, and (on a clear day) views as far south as Gran Canaria. *9km northeast of La Laguna.*

Taganana

This pretty white village is strung out along the hillside, which plunges steeply towards the coast. There are beaches just 2km further north, but these are not suitable for swimming due to their dangerous undertow. *24km northeast of La Laguna.*

Small settlements dot the Anaga Mountains

Drive: Anaga Peninsula

This excursion takes in the highlights of the northeast peninsula, from the green peaks of the Anaga mountains to the golden sands of Playa de las Teresitas. Choose a clear day to get the best from the *miradores* (viewpoints) en route. (This drive may also be combined with the walk on pages 74–5.)

Aim to arrive at the Casa de Carta museum as it opens at 9am, then allow around 3 hours, excluding stops, to reach Las Teresitas beach.

Start from Tacoronte.

1 Tacoronte

This straggling town, 20km east of Puerto de la Cruz, is famous for its wine, and two fine churches: the 17th-century Iglesia de Santa Catalina, and, close by, the Iglesia del Cristo de los Dolores, which holds a much revered 17th-century statue of Christ.
Take the TF122 north, noting the ancient dragon tree as you are leaving town.

2 Casa de Carta (near Valle Guerra)

An excellent ethnographic museum in an 18th-century house (*see p70*). *Continue on the TF122 for 4km, turn right at Tejina onto the TF121 and continue for 12km through Tegueste, Las Canteras and Las Mercedes, stopping to admire the Miradores de Jardina and Cruz del Carmen. After another 1½km, turn left (signposted towards Las Carboneras, start of the walk on p74). Continue straight ahead, past the second Carboneras sign, to Taborno (13km past Cruz del Carmen).*

3 Taborno

This small village is situated high among the Anaga peaks at 1,024m, and consequently enjoys marvellous views of the surrounding area.
Retrace your route to where you turned left towards Las Carboneras. Carry straight on, then rejoin the main TF123 road. This scenic road continues for 8km along the top of the cumbre (ridge), with views to north and south offering a glimpse of the golden sands of Las Teresitas.
Turn off left towards El Bailadero.

4 El Bailadero

A spectacular *mirador* (*see p71*), at which point you can either turn round and go south (left) to Las Teresitas beach and Santa Cruz, go south and then turn north to Taganana (*see p71*), or continue east (straight ahead) for 6km to Chamucadas, where there is another fine mirador. Shortly after this, the road comes to an end.
From El Bailadero head south on the TF112 to San Andrés.

5 Playa de las Teresitas

It is estimated that this golden strip, brought over from the Sahara, represents some four million sackfuls of sand. It is a superb beach with safe, shallow waters and mountain backdrops. It is well maintained, rarely very busy, and is unspoilt by surrounding developments. The adjacent village of San Andrés is renowned for its fish restaurants. Notice its ruined castle, neatly smashed in half by a flood tide some decades ago.
Continue back along the coastal road for 8km to the waterfront of Santa Cruz.

View of the mountains from Pico del Inglés

6 Santa Cruz

Just before you reach the centre of town, look for the Club Náutico (Yacht Club), beside which are the remains of the Castillo de Paso Alto. From here Santa Cruz enjoyed its finest military moment in 1797, repulsing an attack by Admiral Lord Nelson and in the process shooting off the lower part of his right arm.

It is often surprisingly easy to park close to the centre of town on the main road, if you arrive by early evening. The streets come alive again after siesta – a good time to visit the capital.

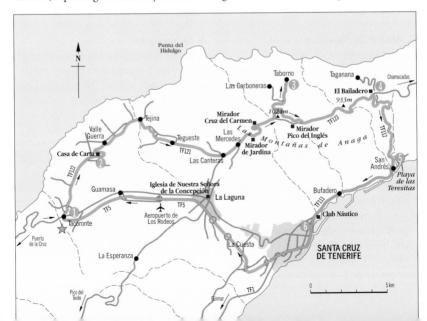

Walk: Chinamada

This walk takes you into the heart of the Anaga Mountains, to a village which, until 1993, was cut off from all roads, and where the inhabitants still live in caves carved into the mountainside. It's an easy walk to follow, and suitable for all ages. Much of the first half could be undertaken in a four-wheel drive vehicle or even an ordinary car, though the track is quite bumpy.

Allow 1½–2 hours.

Start from Las Carboneras (see map p73, on how to get there).

1 Las Carboneras

This small village is made up of two bars, a church, and a handful of houses. *Start by the main plaza and follow the wooden sign, posted to Chinamada (where the road proper finishes and the new track begins).*

2 Roque de Taborno

The first stretch of the walk is dominated by the green, velvety peak of Roque de Taborno, away to your right. This rises to 706m and has a distinctive, bullet-like basalt peak. In winter the wonderful sweet smell of the *retama* plant fills the air along the route.

After about 15 minutes, the track turns around the corner away from Roque de Taborno, but still offers fine views. Hillside caves now begin to appear. Turn the next bend and the first cave houses of Chinamada are to the right-hand side of the track. *Follow the track, which wiggles to the left through a tiny pass and continues ahead.*

3 Barranco del Tomadero

The view to the left of the track, across the deep green ravine that separates Chinamada from the tiny white houses of Batán, is stunning. This ravine runs all the way to the sea at Punta del Hidalgo. Goats graze on these seemingly impossibly steep, terraced slopes, providing meat and cheese for the people of Chinamada.

4 Chinamada

Note the fine dragon tree to the right of the path. A recently-built chapel stands straight ahead of you. The houses of the 30 or so people who live here are small and cut back into the rocky ridge but, as you will see, they are hardly Stone Age. You can walk along the narrow path alongside the houses. If you are feeling inspired by the scenery, it's around an hour's walk all the way down to Punta del Hidalgo (from where buses run back to La Laguna).

Return the short distance to the small crossroads and climb the hill up the steps to the right, signposted *Las Escaleras* (The Stairs).

5 Las Escaleras

The steps don't last for long, descending down to a narrow path. This is a pretty route, strewn with ferns and Canary bell flowers. The path initially skirts the hillside. There's only one route to follow, and a metal conduit runs along the side of the path as a guide.

After about 30 minutes you will see the main road down to your left. At this point you can descend and walk back to the village (half a kilometre), or continue along the path for another 10–15 minutes to the Mirador de las Escaleras, which offers yet another fine aspect of these

Fertile slopes of the Anaga Mountains

majestic hills. Follow the path back and make the descent to the road.

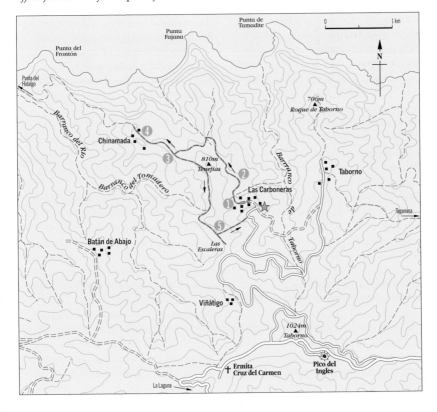

La Laguna

La Laguna (officially San Cristóbal de la Laguna) was founded in 1496 by the island conqueror, Alonso Fernández de Lugo, as capital of all the Canaries. It remained the main city until the early-18th century when the privilege passed to the upstart port of Santa Cruz (*see p66*), and its numerous handsome 16th- and 17th-century mansions attest to the wealth of this era. Despite its wonderful architecture and Spanish atmosphere, it is almost untouched by tourism.

La Laguna cathedral

In 1999, UNESCO declared it a World Heritage Site for its pioneering checkerboard layout: 'the first ideal "city-territory" laid out according to philosophical principles' and the model for many settlements to come in the New World. Today, its university gives it a youthful air in spite of its antiquity.

Because of the grid-pattern street plan, sightseeing here is easy. Start in the unmissable main square of Plaza del Adelantado in front of the *ayuntamiento* (town hall) and pick up a town map from the kiosk which serves as a tourist information office. If you don't have much time, simply walk up Calle Obispo Rey Redondo and return via the parallel street of Calle San Agustín.

Plaza del Adelantado

This is probably the best architectural ensemble in the archipelago. The *ayuntamiento* itself was originally built in 1546 but treated to a Neo-Classical remodelling in the 19th century. To its left is the **Antiguo Colegio de las Dominicas** and to the right the **Monasterio de Santa Catalina de Siena** (a convent dating from the 17th century with an unusual lattice-work gallery), and beyond this the colonial Baroque palace of **Palacio de Nava** (1776). Across the square is the tiny **Ermita de San Miguel**, built in 1507 by order of Lugo, and in one corner the 16th-century **Casa de Anchieta.**

Monasterio de Santa Catalina. Open: Mon–Sat 7–11.45am, Sun 6.30–8pm. Free admission.

Calle Obispo Rey Redondo

This ancient street possesses many fine buildings. Walking up it from Plaza del Adelantado on your left you have the *ayuntamiento*, the **Casa del Corregidor** with shields carved in the stone of its façade, the **Casa del Alhóndiga** (1709) and, on the first corner, the **Casa de Alvarado Bracamonte**. This splendid former residence of the island's Captain Generals dates back to 1631. It now belongs to the city and is open to the public when there is an exhibition on. Go upstairs to see its splendid wooden panelling and its Moorish wooden-trellised oriel window.

A short way on you pass the **cathedral** on your right, a cavernous, awe-inspiring church, founded in 1515, but remodelled in 1904–5. There are many treasures to admire, and behind the High Altar is the simple tomb of de Lugo.

Further up still, the **Teatro Leal** (right), an overbearing pink and yellow confection with two bright red cupolas dating from 1915, faces **the Casa de los Marqueses de Torrehermosa** (18th century) across the street. At the top of the street is the charming Plaza de la Concepción, where lovely old houses look onto a square with two dragon trees, and a bizarre Art Nouveau structure covering an electricity substation. Here also stands the **Iglesia de la Nuestra Señora de la Concepción**, the city's oldest church, with particularly outstanding woodwork inside and a distinctive stone belltower rising above it.

Calle San Agustín

Walking back down this street towards the Plaza del Adelantado, most of the buildings of interest are on the left. First comes the former convent **of San Agustin**, a fine 16th-century ex-

One corner of the Plaza del Adelantado

convent building with a graceful bell tower, now housing the Instituto de Canarias. Next to it is the church and hospital of **Nuestra Señora de los Dolores**. No. 28 is the Bishops Palace in the former **Casa Salazar**, a 17th-century house with a beautiful patio open to the public. Across the side turning of Calle Tabares de Cala is the **Museo de Historia** (*see below*) in the old residence of the Lecaro family. Opposite is the **Casa de los Jesuitas**, a 17th century house formerly the seat of the Jesuit order. Continuing down the street, on the left is the **Casa Montanes** (No.16) occupied by the Consejo Consultivo de Canarias – peep inside to see the perfect patio of this 1746 house. Finally, on the right, forming the corner with Calle Nava y Grimón, is the **Monasterio de San Juan Bautista**, founded in the 16th century but rebuilt in the 18th century after a fire. It is a convent for monks of the Franciscan order of Poor Clares.

Museo de Historia de Tenerife (History Museum)

Tenerife's history museum is housed in the 16th-century Casa Lercaro, a lovely old building with two patios and uneven floors which belonged to a family of nobility and patronage. The exhibits on the first floor cover the development of the island from the Spanish conquest and Christianisation in the 14th and 15th centuries to the present. The museum tells the story of how the first colonists divided up the land and water resources between themselves, cutting down forests and planting crops for home consumption or, where possible, for export. As an island community, the inhabitants of Tenerife depended as little as possible on metropolitan Spain but developed most of the skills they needed – working wood, metals, stone, pottery and textiles. Examples of their craft can be seen here.

Calle San Agustín, 22. Tel: (922) 825949. www.museosdetenerife.org
Open: Tue–Sun 9am–7pm. Admission charge.

Museo de Ciencia y del Cosmos (Museum of Science and the Universe)

The signposting to this museum, happily sited on 'Milky Way Street' on the outskirts of town, could be a lot better but you'll know you are nearly there when you see the large radio telescope parked on the flat roof. It is essentially one large hall of science toys organised into three grand themes: the human body, how things work and the universe. Once a month the museum holds astronomy sessions that are open to the public.

Its star attraction is a tourist trip into space, which takes about twenty minutes and has a commentary available in English. Two virtual personalities greet you, the space tourist, and 'fax' you to three destinations – the comet Neat Q4, Jupiter's volcanically active moon Io, and finally the planet Mars for which you need to don 3-D spectacles – where more ethereal beings act as tour guides and special effects simulate local conditions.

Calle Vía Láctea. Tel: (922) 315265. www.museosdetenerife.org
Open: Tue–Sun 9am–7pm. Admission charge but free on Sun.

The radio telescope on 'Milky Way Street'

Architecture

The first Canarians, the Guanches, had little regard for architectural niceties, using the nearest hole in the wall as a home. Caves at least have the benefit of being cool in summer and warm in winter. Not all Guanches lived in caves, however, and it is quite likely that the first Guanche houses were not unlike the small, white, one-storey dwellings found in the Canarian countryside today. These pueblo-style houses are built of wood, rough rubblework stone, sand and mud.

The Spanish brought colonial-style architecture to the islands, and it still survives in many forms in the older

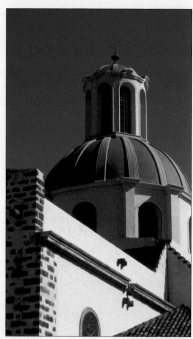

towns of the archipelago. Chief among these towns is La Laguna, on Tenerife, whose old quarter is a showcase of Spanish-Canarian architecture from the 16th and 17th centuries. Sturdy stone mansions with carved coats of arms and beautifully crafted wooden balconies are the exterior hallmarks of a wealthy merchant's or colonist's home. The Canaries are famous for their balconies, and many modern buildings try to turn the clock back with handcrafted appendages. The wood comes from the heart of the Canarian pine tree and is known as *tea* (pronounced tay-ah).

and the provincial town of Teror are the pride of Gran Canaria, and Santa Cruz de la Palma also features notable vernacular domestic architecture.

Church architecture on the islands reflects the Spanish, also colonial style, with two splendid examples of *mudéjar* (Moorish-influenced) ceilings in the principal churches of Santa Cruz de La Palma and La Laguna.

Peer inside the entrance of many an old house and you will find a Moorish-style patio, rich with greenery, perhaps even a fountain and, around the interior, more balconies. The epitome of this style is the Casa de los Balcones in La Orotava, on Tenerife. Elsewhere on Tenerife keep your eyes open in Santa Cruz, Puerto de la Cruz, and Garachico, and do pay a visit to the Casa de la Carta museum, near Valle de Guerre, and the History Museum in La Laguna. The La Vegueta district of Las Palmas

Architectural details from the islands – typical Spanish and Moorish aspects

Valle de Orotava

As the northern slopes of Mount Teide descend to the sea they form a natural, sloping bowl delimited by cliffs on either side. This is the fertile and densely populated Valle de Orotava (Valley of Orotava) which is shared by three towns: the historic La Orotava itself, the brash holiday resort of Puerto de la Cruz on the coast, and the much less distinctive Los Realejos.

Striking pottery in the Museo de Ceramica

This has always been Tenerife's agricultural heartland, producing sugar cane in the past and now mostly bananas, although also increasingly grapes for wine. From La Orotava a scenic road winds upwards, out of the vale through extensive pinewoods towards the Teide national park.

Los Realejos

Los Realejos may be the poor relation to its famous neighbours, La Orotava and Puerto de la Cruz, but it does have at least the first church built on Tenerife, dating from 1496. Nine of the last Guanche leaders, or *menceys*, were baptised here. Several other buildings also date from the 15th and 16th centuries. The municipality extends up the slopes of Mount Teide and there are several nature reserves which are good for walking in.

Mirador de Humboldt

The most easily accessible viewpoint in the Valle de Orotava is this balcony of dressed stone named after the naturalist and traveller Baron Alexander von Humboldt whose ship put into Santa

Cruz in 1799 on the way to South America.
Take exit 31 from the Autopista del Norte motorway and follow the signs for La Orotava through Cuesta de la Villa. The mirador is on a bend on the right.

Museo de Ceramica (Casa Tafuriaste, Pottery Museum)

The much restored early 17th century Casa Tafuriaste serves at once as a pottery workshop and a ceramics museum displaying 1,000 pieces. There are regular demonstrations of the potter's art.
Calle León 3, 2km west of the centre of La Orotava on the La Luz to La Candias road. Tel: (922) 321447. Open: Mon–Sat 10am–6pm, Sun 10am–2pm.

Pueblo Chico

Children will feel at home in this model scene of Canarian landscapes and buildings reproduced at a scale of 1:25 and surrounded by gardens planted with native Canary Islands shrubs and flowers. You enter by a Guanche cave, pass by a model of Tenerife Sur airport with two planes moving along the runway, and the port of Santa Cruz complete with ferry cruising through the water. The upper area presents the most emblematic buildings from all the Canary Islands and includes some surprises, such as a branch of the department store of El Corte Inglés. Throughout there are plenty of details to identify, including miniature dragon trees, banana plants, windmills, salt pans, wrestlers, dolphins and La Orotava flower carpets. Sound effects add life to the models and at night they are illuminated.

Camino Cruz de los Martillos, 62, La Orotava. Take exit (salida) 35 from the Autopista del Norte motorway. Tel: (922) 334060. www.pueblochico.com Open: 9am–7pm daily. Admission charge.

Casa del Vino La Baranda

Tenerife's wines are not well known outside the islands but you can find out all you want to know about them in this 17th century Canarian *hacienda*, La Baranda, just beyond the borders of the Valle de Orotava, which the island's government has turned into a promotional exhibition. Tastings are available and you can buy the wines in the shop. There is also a restaurant on the premises (*see p160*) serving innovative Canarian food and traditional recipes.

From the Autopista del Norte take the exit for El Sauzal. Tel: (922) 572535. www.cabtfe.es/casa-vino Open: Tue–Sat 10am–10pm, Sun 11am–6pm. Admission free.

Grapes are now a common sight in the Valle de Orotava

La Orotava

La Orotava is one of the very few towns in the Canaries that has conserved its historical centre intact. Since tourism began in the 19th century it has been an essential stop for visitors to the island. The centre is a compact mass of handsome buildings but among them are some pretty squares and two sizeable public gardens. An industrious place, La Orotava could claim to be the craft centre of Tenerife and its many small shops are good places to look for souvenirs.

Iglesia de Nuestra Señora de la Concepción

During the Corpus Christi celebrations (in May or June) some of the streets and squares are decorated with ornate 'carpets' using flower petals and coloured volcanic sands.

Casa de los Balcones (House of the Balconies)

This quintessential and most famous Canarian building is named after the superbly crafted balconies on the façade and overlooking the courtyard. It is now a craft and gift shop with its own brand of gifts that are sold in tourist resorts and airports throughout the island. The tropical patio, full of exotic greenery, an ancient winepress, old pictures and pottery, conjures up an evocative atmosphere of early colonial days. The house dates from the 1630s and was the home to a wealthy family: a museum in it has displays on 17th century daily life. The Casa del Turista, opposite, is also a craft and gift shop run by the same company and with the same opening hours. It is slightly older, having being completed in 1593. There is a good view from its terrace.
Calle San Francisco, 3. Tel: (922) 330629. www.casa-balcones.com
Open: Mon–Sat 8.30am–7.30pm, Sun 8.30am–1.30pm.

Casa Torrehermosa

This old colonial house is now the official outlet for Tenerife-made crafts.
Calle Tomás Zerolo, 27. Tel: (922) 304013. www.artenerife.com
Open: Mon–Fri 9.30am–6.30pm, Sat 9.30am–2pm. Free admission.

Museo de Artesania Iberoamericana (Museum of Spanish-American Crafts)

Across the road from the Casa Torrehermosa, in the Convento de Santo Domingo, is this small museum of Spanish and Latin American arts and crafts.
Calle Tomás Zerolo, 34. Tel: (922) 352906. Open: Mon–Sat 9.30am–6pm. Admission charge.

Hijuela del Botánico

This 'Offshoot of the Botanic Garden', is connected to its famous 'parent' nearby in Puerto de la Cruz (*see p88*). It is a small, densely planted area claiming over 3,000 different tropical and subtropical species.

Calle Hermano Apolinar. Open: daily dawn–dusk. Free admission.

Hospital de la Santísima Trinidad (Hospital of the Holy Trinity)

Formerly an 18th-century convent, this is now a hospital for mentally handi-capped patients. The revolving drum set into the main door was to allow people to donate gifts anonymously. There is a good view over the Valle de Orotava from the terrace outside the door of the hospital.

Calle San Francisco. Tel: (922) 330200.

Iglesia de Nuestra Señora de la Concepción (Church of Our Lady of the Immaculate Conception)

Along with its namesake in La Laguna, this is probably one of the finest churches on the island. It is an extravagant, handsome, Baroque structure built between 1768 and 1788, with twin onion-topped towers and a large dome. Its screen, altar, statuary and carved choir stalls are regarded as masterpieces.

Plaza Casañas. Tel: (922) 330187. Open: usually for mass only.

Moorish balconied homes in La Orotava

Walk: La Orotava

La Orotava's steep cobbled streets are perfect for strolling around. They are lined with 17th and 18th century houses distinguished by their elegantly carved wooden balconies and often concealing charming patios. Several of these buildings now contain craft shops, cafes and restaurants.

Start on the lower side of Plaza de la Constitución, across the square from the church, the Iglesia de San Agustín. Allow 1½ hours.

1 Carrera del Escultor Estévez.

From the square, go up this, the main street through the old part of town, passing the yellow half-timbered 18th-century building that houses the tourist office on your right (No. 2, on the corner of Tomás Zerolo). On the left, above Libreria Miranda, is the birthplace of the sculptor Fernando Estévez, after whom the street is named. Follow the road along the side of the Plaza del Ayuntamiento, with the big pink town hall across the square to your left. No. 17, the former Casa Benítez de Lugo, now the **Hotel Rural La Oratava**, has a café in its delightful courtyard.

2 Calle San Francisco

Turn left into the short, steep Calle San Francisco.

Immediately on your left is the **Casa de los Balcones** (No. 3). No. 5 is also a historical building with a delightful patio. Opposite, is the **Renaissance Casa del Turista** (No. 4).

3 Plaza de San Francisco

This brings you into the steeply sloping, Plaza de San Francisco, a triangular space with two dragon trees – one spindly, one squat – planted towards the top end. On the right are the **Iglesia de San Francisco** and **Hospital de la Santísima Trinidad**.

4 Hijuela del Jardin Botanico

Turn right at the bottom of Plaza de San Francisco down Calle Hermano Apolinar.

This takes you along the side of the botanical garden, the Hijuela del Jardin Botanico, a delightful rectangle crammed with foliage.

5 Iglesia de la Concepción

Turn left past the entrance of the garden, down Calle Tomás Pérez. Cross Carrera del Escultor Estévez.

On the left is the 18th century casino, converted into a library. This brings you to the church of **Nuestra Señora de la Concepción** with its squashed striped onion domes.

6 Calle Tomás Zerolo

From the square by the church turn right down Calle Inocencio Garcia.

Towards the end of it is **Casa Salazar**, an asymmetrical, yellow and cream, Art Nouveau-cum-Neo-Gothic building with floral frills, a central balcony and a wrought iron *mirador* to one side. Detour left down Calle Tomás Zerolo to visit the **Museo de Artesania Iberoamericana** in the old convent of Santo Domingo and, opposite, the craft shop in the **Casa Torrehermosa**.

Sunset over La Orotava

7 Plaza de la Constitución

Return up Tomás Zerolo and continue across Carrera del Escultor Estévez. Turn left on to Calle San Agustin and you enter the top of Plaza de la Constitución.

This is looked down upon by a handsome red building set in immaculate gardens, the **Liceo de Taoro,**

the seat of a society dedicated to the promotion of the arts and culture. Beside it are **Jardines Marquesado de la Quinta Roja**, a series of terraces of ornamental plants around a 19th century mausoleum.

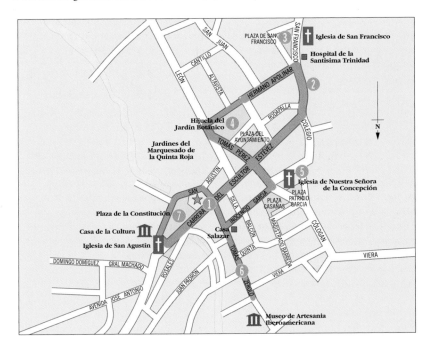

Puerto de la Cruz

Puerto de la Cruz, or Puerto, as it is known, is the longest-established and most complete holiday resort on Tenerife. It has a magnificent backdrop, with Teide towering above, and the lush Orotava Valley sweeping down to the city.

Bird of Paradise at Bananera el Guanche

Unlike most Canarian resorts, this is a town with its own identity, where locals still live, work, eat and drink. The British put Puerto on the map as a holiday destination around a century ago, and so it has stayed. In addition to its old-world charms, such as the 17th-century Customs House and the pedestrian promenade at St Telmo which shouldn't be missed, it also features some high-quality visitor attractions on its outskirts.

Puerto de la Cruz is 40km southwest of Santa Cruz. Tourist office: Plaza de Europa. Tel: (922) 386000. Open: Mon–Fri 9am–8pm, Sat 9am–1pm.

Bananera el Guanche

Despite its obvious mass tourist appeal, the cultivation of this miniature banana plantation is well explained, and its lush, terraced gardens hold an extensive range of indigenous and exotic plants. There is an area of over 400 cacti, and a small collection of farmyard animals.

3km southeast of Puerto on La Orotava road. Tel: (922) 331853.
www.bananeraelguanche.com
Open: daily 9am–6pm. Admission charge.
Free bus from Playa Martiánez.

Jardín Botánico (Botanic Garden)

This is the oldest of Puerto's attractions, founded in 1788 by King Carlos III as a halfway house Jardín de Aclimatación (Acclimatisation Garden) for plants travelling from the tropics to Spain. It's a small, shady place with over 200 species of plants and trees crowding into just 2.5 hectares. Most people's favourite is the giant 200-year-old South American fig tree in the centre, a menacing gothic mass of intertwined roots and branches.

Jardín Botánico: 2km southeast of the town centre, Calle Retama. Tel: (922) 383572. Open: daily 9am–6pm. Admission charge.

Lago Martiánez (Lake Martiánez)

Until the opening of Puerto's Playa Jardín, the Lido Martiánez was the town's unofficial 'beach'. It was designed by Lanzarote artist César Manrique in 1969, and brilliantly solved the problem of the beachless seafront. There are several swimming pools and a large lake with an island in the middle.

Avenida de Colón, Playa Martiánez. Tel: (922) 383852. Open: daily 9am–6pm. Admission charge.

Loro Parque (Parrot Park)

This Florida-style wildlife park maintains very high standards of both conservation and entertainment. Set in

superb tropical gardens, it was conceived as a parrot park, and is said to contain the world's largest collection of parrots. It has also recently added the largest dolphinarium outside America, a huge aquarium with sharks which claims the largest underwater tunnel in the world, a gorilla jungle, and a bat cave. Other attractions include a 180-degree special effects cinema, parrot shows, and performing sea lions. There are crocodiles, tigers, and the biggest penguinarium in the world.
Calle San Felipe, 3km west of the town centre in the Punta Brava district. Tel: (922) 373841. www.loroparque.com

Open: daily 8.30am–6.45pm. Admission charge. Bus: free from Playa Martiánez & Playa de las Américas every 20 minutes.

Playa Jardín
This new black-sand beach was opened in 1992–3. The crashing Atlantic waves have been tamed by a man-made reef comprising some 4,000 20-tonne concrete blocks (submerged out of sight), and the back of the beach area was landscaped under the direction of César Manrique. Adjacent is the 17th-century Castillo de San Felipe, which has been re-opened as a cultural centre.
Open: Mon–Fri 10am–1pm, 6–9pm.

A colourful mural at Bananera el Guanche

Bananas

The banana plant, such a typical sight in the north of Gran Canaria and Tenerife, is technically a herb rather than a tree. It is native to Malaysia and was being eaten as long ago as the 6th century BC. Gradually its cultivation reached India before being spread through Africa by Arab traders. In the early 16th century Portuguese explorers introduced it to the Canary Islands, where the wetter parts of the islands were perfect for supplying the high amounts of water demanded by a thirsty plant. At the end of the 19th century the banana supplanted the dwindling sugar cane industry and established itself as the islands' most popular crop.

Despite its apparent success, however, the banana is in gradual decline. Most European markets reject bananas from the Canaries because they are smaller than those produced elsewhere, and almost the entire crop (some 400,000 tonnes a year) has to be sold to mainland Spain. Growers believe that the rest of the world has got it wrong.

Eat a banana here, they say, and you'll never want to try one anywhere else: small bananas have a superior smell and taste and their nutritional and cosmetic qualities are more concentrated.

The banana is truly nature's fast food, being easily peeled and eaten (either raw or cooked). Originally bananas contained large seeds but these were selectively bred out of the hybrids planted commercially, which are propagated asexually – a 'sucker' being used to start the next plant. Bananas grow in huge bunches with the fruits arranged on them in tiers (or 'hands'). The plants demand large quantities of water.

Not only are bananas easy to eat but they are healthy eating, being a good source of energy and rich in iron, magnesium, vitamin B6 and potassium – for which they are sometimes recommended to people with high blood pressure. They are said to be easy to digest and good for digestive disorders, both diarrhoea and constipation.

Many farmers in the Canaries are diversifying into a range of other crops including: tropical fruits, such as avocados, papaya and mangoes; cut flowers; ornamental plants (there is a big demand for these from new hotels and tourist developments); aloe vera; citrus fruits; wine-grapes; and even, on Gran Canaria, a little coffee. But it is likely to be a long while yet before the banana plantation ceases to be a typical sight in the Canary Islands countryside. The banana is still the biggest crop, with Tenerife leading the other islands in annual production.

The banana has long been an important crop to the Canary Islands, with plantations a common sight

Walk: Puerto de la Cruz

Puerto de la Cruz remains at heart a Spanish colonial town with many tangible reminders of its past. This walk will show you a little of the town's history and architecture. Avoid Monday if you want to visit the Archaeological Museum.

Allow 1–1½ hours (excluding time spent in the Museum).

Start from the El Peñon (the Rock) religious monument, next to the football stadium.

1 Calle de San Felipe

This is a charming old street of one-storey fishermen's houses, and some good local restaurants. Look out for the unusual green oriel window at No. 16.
Turn left into Calle de Pérez Zamora, and left again into Calle de Lomo.

2 Calle de Lomo

The **Museo Arqueológico**
(Archaeological Museum. *Tel: (922) 209317. Open: Tue–Sat 10am–1pm & 6–9pm, Sun 10am–1pm. Admission charge.*) is housed in a fine 19th-century mansion. It stages temporary exhibitions.
Retrace your steps to Calle de San Felipe and continue in the direction you were walking in.

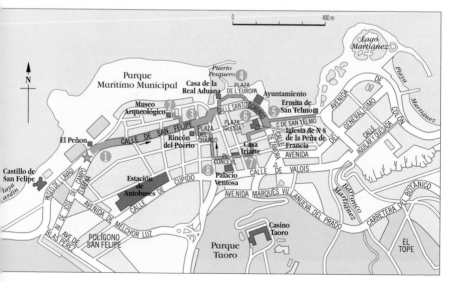

3 Plaza del Charco
This handsome square marks the centre of the town. Look into the Rincón del Puerto, a fine, typically Canarian balconied courtyard, built in 1739.
Leave the square by Calle La Marina to reach the port.

4 Puerto Pesquero (Fishing Port)
To the right-hand side of the port, the beautiful black and white stone house is the Casa de la Real Aduana (Royal Custom House), the oldest building in town, dating from 1620. Note the fortifications to the seaward side. On the opposite side of the street is the Casa Miranda, dating from around 1730.

A little further on is a new square with cannons, the Plaza de l'Europa, from which there are good sea views. To the right are the Casas Consistoriales (town hall offices, built in 1973).
Go a short way up Calle Santo Domingo and then turn left on to Calle de San Telmo.

5 Calle de San Telmo
The start of this promenade is known as the Punta del Viento (Windy Point), marked by a modern sculpture of a windswept girl. Below, the waves break spectacularly into the black-lava rockpools. The tiny, snow-white **Ermita de San Telmo** (Church of St Elmo) dates from the 18th century.
Retrace your steps to the start of the promenade; continue on for a few yards then turn right into Calle La Hoya, which leads to Plaza de la Iglesia.

6 Plaza de la Iglesia
Note the old-fashioned *bodega* (wine-

Strolling in Puerto de la Cruz

shop) on the left before entering the square. This is Puerto's loveliest plaza, with an elegant swan fountain in the centre. The **Iglesia de Nuestra Señora de la Peña de Francia** is a beautiful 16th-century building with Baroque altarpieces and side-chapels. The **Hotel Marquesa** (1712), and the **Hotel Monopol** (1742), also on the square, both possess typical balconied patios.
Leave the Plaza by Calle Cólogan and take the second street, Calle Iriarte (right).

7 Casa Iriarte
An 18th-century house with a balcony onto the street, and a lovely interior patio. It houses craft-sellers (mostly embroidery), and a small naval museum.
Tel: (922) 383311. Open: Mon–Sat 9.30–7pm. Admission charge.

8 Palacio Ventosa
On the pretty square diagonally opposite the Casa Iriarte is the Colegio San Agustín. This occupies the 18th-century **Palacio Ventosa**, of which the most notable feature is the tall tower. It is not open to the public.
Turn right into Calle de Blanco. This leads back to the Plaza del Charco.

Western Tenerife

The northwest corner and west coast of Tenerife are highly rewarding areas to explore. The countryside of the Teno Hills is as beautiful as any scenery to the northeast; Icod de los Vinos has a famous old dragon tree and Garachico is undeniably one of the island's most charming small towns.

An old lava stream at Garachico

Garachico

What at first sight looks like a modest fishing port turns out to be an outstanding collection of old buildings arranged along narrow, cobbled streets. Surprisingly the town is a reconstruction, as in 1706 it was all but destroyed by lava flowing down to the sea. To appreciate how Garachico was rebuilt on the lava peninsula that formed here, approach it from El Tanque and you will get a splendid bird's-eye view.

The most notable survivor of the disaster is the beautifully preserved seafront **Castillo de San Miguel** (Castle of St Michael), which dates from the 16th century. It now houses a small museum of fossils and shells. Nearby is the port, which until 1706 was the most important in Tenerife because of its fine natural harbour. On the town side is a charming square with a beautiful sunken garden. A 16th-century arch and a 17th-century winepress adorn this flower-filled space. From here there is a view of the 18th-century **Iglesia de Santa Ana** (Church of St Anna).

The town's most beautiful church is the 16th-century **Iglesia de San Francisco** (Church of St Francis) on the main square. The old convent next door now houses a cultural centre, **Casa de Cultura**. At the other end of town is the 17th-century Convento de Santo Domingo, now home to the **Museo de Arte Contemporaneo** (Museum of Contemporary Art).

31km west of Puerto de la Cruz. Castillo de San Miguel. Tel: (922) 830000. Open: daily 9am–6pm. Admission charge. Casa de Cultura, Plaza de San Francisco. Tel: (922) 830001. Open: Mon–Fri 8am–1pm & 4–7pm, Sat & Sun 8am–1pm. Museo de Arte Contemporaneo, Plaza Santo Domingo. Tel: (922) 830000. Open: Mon–Fri 10am–1pm & 4–6pm. Admission charge.

Icod de los Vinos

Icod de los Vinos is famous for its 1,000-year-old dragon tree, the Drago Milenario. The real age of this monster is not known – some estimates put it as old as 1,500 years – but it is certainly the oldest dragon tree in existence. It is also the largest, being 17m tall with a girth of 20m. Its 300 branches are estimated to weigh 80 tonnes and its trunk another 65 tonnes. To protect this singular tree the island government and town council have built a park around it, the Parque del Drago, which is planted with native Canary Island species.

20km west of Puerto de la Cruz.
Parque del Drago. Tel: (922) 814510.
Open: daily 9.30am–6.30pm. Admission charge.

Puerto de Santiago and Los Gigantes

A quiet, low-rise, up-market holiday development has sprung up here to take advantage of the dramatic sea-cliff setting of Los Gigantes, and the black sandy beach next to Puerto de Santiago. Massive cliffs drop almost sheer into the sea from a height of 500m.

42km north of Playa de las Américas.

Masca

The tip of the northwest is covered by the Teno Hills – one of the most picturesque corners of the island, rent by deep ravines, and cloaked in lush greenery. The road south from Buenavista del Norte passes along steep, narrow hairpin-bends, and leads to the village of Masca. Until recently it was virtually 'undiscovered', but now Masca is on most coach excursion itineraries. Despite the occasional crowds, however, its magical site cannot be diminished. Its houses are set on narrow ridges which plunge down into a verdant valley of dramatic rock formations.

20km southwest of Garachico via Buenavista del Norte.

Hotel La Quinta Roja, Garachico

Parque Nacional del Teide

At 3,718m, the dormant volcano of Mount Teide is the highlight of Tenerife in every sense, but you need a good day to get the best out of a visit. Weather conditions in the national park vary dramatically and can be very different to those down on the coast. It is not unusual to set off on a nice day at sea level, plunge into low cloud on your way up, and emerge into bright blue skies when you get above, say 1,500 metres. In winter, snow falls, gale-force winds blow, and the roads and cable car are sometimes closed. In summer, daytime temperatures can soar above 40°C, although the summit of Teide will still feel chilly and may not be cloud free. If you are not tied to a particular day, check the forecast on the morning before you set off and postpone your visit if necessary.

A LITTLE HISTORY

About three million years ago, a giant volcano near the present Mount Teide (but much, much bigger) exploded and/or collapsed in on itself. The volcano walls, or what was left of them, formed a *caldera* (crater) in which Teide and other volcanoes now stand. The *caldera* measures 48km in circumference, and some parts of the wall still stand up to 500m high. It may be impossible to visualise this from ground level, but as you gaze upon the torn and twisted earth, try to imagine the awesome power that turned the earth into this alien lunarscape.

Visiting the National Park

There are two visitor information centres: at El Portillo, if you are approaching from La Orotava, Puerto de la Cruz or La Laguna; and in the *parador* at the other side of the park. There are several marked hiking trails to follow, but even if you are only going to do a little walking, go well-shod, well prepared and take a good map with you.

Before you set off, however, you may want to decide whether or not to climb to the summit. The cable car takes you almost to the top of the mountain but, with prior permission, you can ascend to the crater itself. This must be applied for in advance by telephoning (922) 290129 and you must go to the national park office in Santa Cruz de Tenerife (Calle Emilio Calzadilla, No. 4, 5th floor) in person with your passport to sign an agreement accepting responsibility for your own safety.

El Portillo Visitors Information Centre

This information office is

near the northeast entrance to the park. It has a small exhibition on the wildlife within the park area and a botanical garden outside which aims to show the majority of the unusual plants that are native to the Teide area – although don't expect to see much life here until well into spring (April or May). Guided walking tours set off on various routes from El Portillo. They are free of charge but you will need to telephone in advance to book a place.

Adjacent to the junction of TF21 and TF24. Tel: (922) 356000. Open: daily 9am–4pm.

El Teleférico (Cable Car)

This is the only way to get near to the summit of Teide. It ascends from 2,356m to 3,555m in eight minutes. The remaining walk, some 163m to the top, may only be undertaken with permission. At the summit is an iron cross, a sulphurous smell, and (on an exceptionally clear day), views of all the other islands and sometimes North Africa. The cable car does not operate when it is too windy (frequently in winter), and in summer there can be long queues.

Tel: (922) 010445. Weather permitting the cable car operates between 9am–4pm.

Snowy mountains in Mount Teide National Park

Drive: Mount Teide National Park

A main road, the TF21, traverses the park from southwest to northeast with frequent viewpoints provided to stop and admire the grand, dramatic landscapes which have inspired makers of futuristic films to use them as sets for other worlds. The route is just as good a drive in either direction but here it is assumed you are coming up from the south or west.

1 Boca de Tauce

The roads from Arona and Puerto Santiago converge at the crossroads of Boca de Tauce from which there are good views of the mountain. To get there the Puerto Santiago road crosses beds of black crumbled lava left by the 1798 eruption.

2 Llano de Ucanca

From here the road runs across the Llano (plain) de Ucanca, a dusty desert with big clumps of bushes. This is one of the park's many *cañadas* – yellow sedimentary plains where fine debris has accumulated. To the right and ahead are the great crags and cliffs that form the

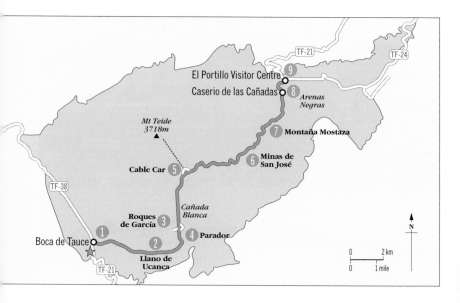

wall of the *caldera*. At the edge of the plain is a group of rocks known as Los Azulejos, which glint green and blue because of iron hydrate deposits.

3 Roques de García
A car park to the left of the road, the Mirador de La Ruleta, serves the park's best known rock formation, a spectacular grouping of pyroclastic debris which is on every coach tour itinerary and often swarming with day-trippers.
There's a relatively easy, circular walking route around the rocks of 3.5km which should take about 2 hours.

4 Parador
Across the road from the rocks is the *parador* which incorporates a cafeteria and Cañada Blanca's visitor information centre, with displays on man's relationship with the area enclosed by the national park.

5 Cable Car
The road from the parador runs straight across the plain of Cañada Blanca and turns sharply along the base of the mountain. A left turning leads to the cable car bottom station.

6 Minas de San José
Past the cable car the road climbs and winds through reddy-brown rocks reminiscent of ploughed earth and descends to this area which is composed of smooth hillocks and slopes of brown gravel.

7 Montaña Mostaza
The road continues to descend and curves round this beautiful volcanic cone.

Llano de Ucanca

8 Caserio de las Cañadas
This group of (usually busy) restaurants can come as a surprise or a relief after such a long trek across the park's bleak lunar landscapes.

9 El Portillo Visitor Centre
The park's other information centre is a few more curves down the road. There is an easy route you can walk from here to see a volcanic cone, Arenas Negras.
The length is 7km and you should allow 3 hours.

THE VOLCANO WITHIN A VOLCANO
About three million years ago, a giant volcano near the site of the present Mount Teide – but much, much bigger – exploded or collapsed in on itself leaving half a massive *caldera* (crater) 48km in circumference and with almost sheer walls of up to 500m. Out of this natural amphitheatre subsequently arose a new volcano, Mount Teide.

The East Coast

The east coast of Tenerife is relatively uninteresting but it has two points of interest worth pulling off the motorway to see. One is the Canary Islands' most popular shrine. The other is the extraordinary complex of ancient and mysterious pyramids discovered at Güimar. Towards the coast's southern end are two small holiday resorts and a famous place to eat fish.

Stepped pyramids, Güimar

Candelaria

At the end of the 14th century (around a hundred years before the Spanish conquest of Tenerife), a Gothic statue of the Virgin Mary was found by the Guanches on the coast of Güimar. They venerated it as Chaxiraxi (Lady of the

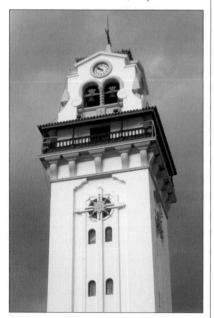
Basílica de Nuestra Señora de Candelaria

World) and the colonists in turn worshipped it as their most holy relic until it was destroyed in a flood in 1826. The church of Candelaria now contains a copy of the original statue by Fernando Estévez. The shrine of Candelaria was built in 1959 to house the statue and is the most important place of pilgrimage in the Canary Islands. More impressive than the church are the nine giant bronze statues of the last Guanche chieftains (*menceys*) by José Abad.

The Pyramids of Güimar

When six pyramids were discovered in a suburb of Güimar, archaeologists dismissed them as mere piles of stones removed from fields by farmers and stacked out of the way of the plough. But on visiting the site in 1991, the anthropologist and explorer Thor Heyerdahl was convinced that the structures really were ancient pyramids built in a similar fashion to those of ancient Mexico, Peru and Mesopotamia. Scientific research produced evidence to support him: these were no random heaps of unwanted stones but elaborately made platforms sited on pre-levelled ground and ascended by steps on their western sides, suggesting an astronomical function.

The site has been superbly equipped for visitors with concrete paths between the pyramids and an audiovisual show in various languages to put them into context. Who built the pyramids, when, and for what reason remain mysteries. Before excavations at Güimar, the ancient inhabitants of the Canary Islands were not thought to have possessed the necessary skills. Heyerdahl was sure that the pyramids were proof of communication between the disparate cultures of the ancient world long before Europeans crossed the Atlantic, but in opening the site to the public he insisted that every visitor be encouraged to keep an open mind.
Calle Chacona, Guimar. Tel: (922) 514510. www.piramidesdeguimar.net Open: daily 9.30am–9pm. Admission charge.

El Médano

This small, developing resort is said to have the best beach in Tenerife – two kilometres of sand lapped by a shallow sea, but it also experiences fearsome winds which are excellent for windsurfing.
22km east of Los Cristianos.

Los Abrigos

The only reason for stopping here – but it is a good one – is to eat in one of a number of fish restaurants for which the little village is renowned.
15km east of Los Cristianos.

Las Galletas and Costa del Silencio

Near the southern tip of the island is the encouragingly named 'Coast of Silence' at a discreet distance from the commotion of Los Cristianos/Playa de las Americas round the corner.
10km southeast of Los Cristianos.

Traditional tile work in Candelaria

Playa de las Américas & Los Cristianos

The south coast of Tenerife is synonymous with the mega-resort. It is the second largest resort in the Canary Islands after Maspalomas on Gran Canaria, and was formed by the fusion of the old harbour of Los Cristianos and the brash new Playa de las Américas. These two now run seamlessly into each other and the built up area continues further as Costa Adeje, consisting principally of San Eugenio and Fañabé. Nearby are several worthwhile commercial tourist attractions.

Outdoor café in Los Cristianos

If you need to escape from all this, La Caleta, 10km north of Playa de las Américas, is one of the best places on the island to sample the local fish and it has a pleasant beach as well.
Los Cristianos is 17km west of Reina Sofía (Tenerife Sur) airport.

Los Cristianos

With the benefit of having a little history and surrounding a working harbour used by a mixture of fishing boats, pleasure craft and ferries chugging to and from La Gomera, Los Cristianos draws a slightly older clientele than Playa de las Américas.
Tourist information: Centro Cultural de Los Cristianos Tel: (922) 757137. Open: Mon–Fri 9am–3.30pm, Sat 9am–1pm.

Playa de las Américas

The boom-town resort of Playa de las Américas was built in the late 1960s as a home-from-home for north European package holidaymakers. There is little that is Canarian, and unless you are happy drinking pints of British beer and eating 'international food', then this place probably isn't for you. The beaches are of dark sand.
Tourist information: Centro Comercial 'City Center' (in front of Parque Santiago II), Playa de las Américas. Tel: (922) 797668. Open: Mon–Fri 9am–9pm, Sat 9am–5pm.

Costa Adeje

The resort's northern extension has six beaches with the harbour Puerto Colón roughly in the middle.
Tourist information: Calle Rafael Puig de Lluvina, 1 (on the Playa de Troya), San Eugenio. Tel: (922) 750633. Open: Mon–Fri 9am–5pm.

Aqualand Costa Adeje

As well as providing pools, slides, islands and bridges galore to splash around in and on, this waterpark also puts on two daily dolphin shows.
Avda. de Austria, 15 Urbanización, San Eugenio Alto, Tel: (922) 715266.

Admission charge. Free bus services from Playa de las Américas and Los Cristianos.

Jardines del Atlantico Bananera

The guided tour of this family farm lasts about an hour and provides lots of information on Tenerife's agriculture. There is a restaurant serving meals made from homegrown ingredients (open 12 noon–4pm).
Near Buzanada. Tel: (922) 720403. Daily tours: 10am, 11.30am, 1pm, 3.30pm & 4.15pm. Admission charge.

Parque Las Águilas

A lush park that specialises in flying displays by birds, but also offers a metal bobsleigh run (for an additional charge) and an assault course. There are exotic bird shows at 11am and 2pm, but the main attraction is the performance of the eagles at noon and 4pm.
Urbanización del Teide. Tel: (922) 729010. Open: daily 10am–6pm. Admission charge. Free bus from Las Americas and Los Cristianos.

Exotic Park

This zoo-cum-gardens is divided into four parts: Cactus and Animal Park (claimed to be the largest cactus collection in the world), Amazonia ('the only rainforest in Europe'), Jurassic Land and Butterfly-Garden. It aims to show animals in their natural habitats rather than putting on cute shows.
Autopista del Sur exit (salida) 26. Tel: (922) 795424. Open: daily 10am–7pm. Admission charge. Free bus service from Los Cristianos.

Mountains protect the habour at Los Cristianos

Walk: Barranco del Infierno

Despite the name ('Hell's Ravine'), this small, steep-sided valley within easy reach of Los Cristianos/Playa de las Américas is a magnet for walkers and is the most visited nature reserve on the island after Mount Teide. It is so popular that visitor numbers have to be limited to 200 at any one time to preserve the fragile ecosystem. Phone (922) 782885 to book your visit a day before you intend to go; but be warned that in heavy rain – or if there is a danger of it – the *barranco* is closed.

The barranco is at the top of Adeje town (6km north of Playa de las Américas). If you arrive by car, park on the steep street, Calle el Molino, as close to Restaurante Otelo as you can.

The walk (there and back) is 6.3 kilometres, for which you are advised to allow 3 hours. The path is well marked and well-trodden with no possible way of getting lost. It climbs 200 metres and can be steep in places. It is wise to wear suitable footwear for walking and a hat, and to carry water with you. Pets are not allowed. There is an admission charge, although the walk is free on Sundays.

The Barranco del Infierno is the only place in the arid landscape of southern Tenerife with running water. As such it

The stunning views from the *barranco* (above and right)

was highly prized by Spanish colonists, who built a channel to feed irrigation ditches and to power the machinery of the old Casa Fuerte sugar refinery in Adeje. The path you follow was made by the workers who built the channel and aqueducts, although they were probably following the ancient track of Guanche goat-herders as archaeological remains of human presence have been found in the ravine. However, you won't strike water until half way along the route.

The route begins at the gate between Restaurante Otelo and the ticket/information kiosk. If you don't want to do the walk, or if you haven't remembered to book a time, you can get a good view of the first part of the *barranco* from a stonebuilt balcony or from the restaurant terrace.

As well as being of great scenic beauty, the *barranco* is of botanical importance because of the variety of plants that grow here. Many of them are native to the Canary Islands and a few grow nowhere else except in this corner of Tenerife. The route can be divided into two starkly contrasting parts: dry and wet.

The first part of the route is across arid slopes supporting a scattering of plants adapted to survival with a little water. A common plant here is the *taraiba*, a member of the euphorbia family, but there are also clumps of gorse and juniper as well as spindle-trees, dragon trees and the occasional wild olive. Foreign invaders include the spiky prickly pear cactus and the agave or century plant. On the higher slopes, forests of Canary pine take over.

Later on during the walk, the path plunges into the humid *barranco* and follows the stream which feeds a dense growth of moisture-loving plants. As you get nearer the waterfall which marks the end of the walk, the vegetation thickens until it verges on rich, moisture-hoarding laurisilva woodland. *Return the way you have come.*

La Gomera

La Gomera is a dome-shaped island with a sunken central plateau, its sides rent by great gullies which almost completely segment it. This tortuous terrain once presented great communication problems and still adds to journey times. The island may be only 23km by 25km at its widest points, but you won't be able to drive round it comfortably in a day, and a minimum of two days is required to see all the island's highlights.

Balconied house in San Sebastián

It would be a shame not to stay overnight on Gomera, since here are arguably two of the best hotels in the Canaries. This really is a case of quality against quantity as, aside from these two, there are only a few other small hotels and pensions. The lack of tourism here constitutes at least half of the

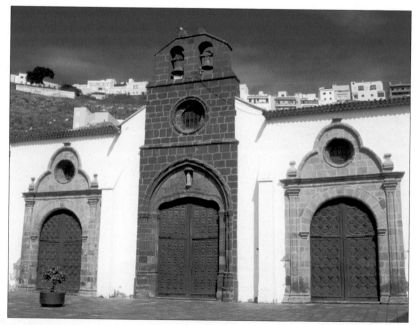

Church façade in San Sebastián

appeal to the island's small group of admirers, although with the increased ferry and flight connections to Tenerife, La Gomera is fast becoming a hiker's and nature-lover's paradise. The comparison between La Gomera and Los Cristianos, just 32km and 35 minutes away by hydrofoil, reveals two wholly different cultures. With only one real beach on the whole of La Gomera, and a limited tourism infrastructure, it seems unlikely that this will change much.

First impressions here are misleading. The barren landscape around San Sebastián soon gives way to some of the most beautiful, luxuriant valleys in the archipelago, while the centre of the island is almost permanently covered in mist, refreshing the prehistoric national park rainforest.

There are few sights as such on Gomera, but natural beauty is here in abundance. To get the best from the island, bring your walking boots and stay for a week.

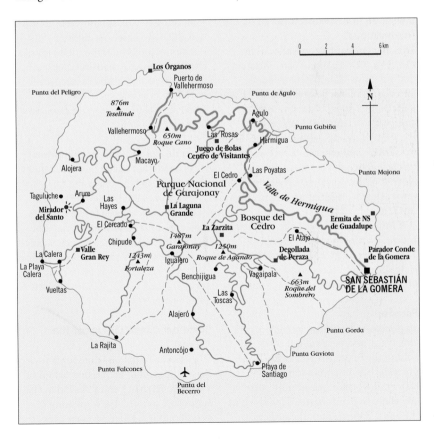

San Sebastián

Your first view of La Gomera, from the ferry, will be of the island capital, San Sebastián. Although the town is famous for its brief association with Columbus (he sailed from here in 1492) it makes light of it and there are few exhibits or memorabilia of the era.

Tourist office: Calle Real, 4. Tel: (922) 140109. Open: 9am–1pm & 4–6pm (summer), 9am–1.30pm & 3.30–6pm (winter).

The harbour and town

Iglesia de la Asunción (Church of the Assumption)

This ancient church on Calle del Medio is the one site in San Sebastián that we know Columbus visited. Records tell us he prayed here in 1492, even though most of the present church dates from the 16th century. It's a fine building, with beautiful woodwork, notably the ceiling and the balcony above the entrance doors. Note, too, the mural depicting the town's defence against an English fleet in 1734.

A little further along Calle del Medio is the Casa Colón/Casa Columbina. The veracity of a Columbus connection is doubtful here, but occasionally the house stages Columbus exhibitions.

Parador

Step into the beautiful *parador* courtyard, and peeping out from behind the luxuriant plants you'll see portraits of Columbus and other historical worthies. Here, more than anywhere in San Sebastián, the spirit of the age is conjured up. It comes as

something of a disappointment to learn that this state hotel was built in 1973. It is a glorious reproduction of a typical aristocratic island mansion, but has no historical pedigree whatsoever (*see pp163–4*).
Lomo de la Horca (signposted from the harbour).

Pozo de Colón (Well of Columbus)

It is known that Columbus's men took water from La Gomera to the New World, and as the hole in the ground here is the nearest well to the harbour, logic has it that this must be 'the well that baptised America'. The well is only accessible through the old Casa del Pozo de la Aguada (House of the Well), formerly the Custom House, and now the Tourist Office.

Torre del Conde (Tower of the Count)

This sturdy pink and white brick tower was built in 1447 by the first Count of Gomera, Hernán Peraza the Elder. His namesake son became something of a tyrant and was killed by Guanches at

the Degollada de Peraza (*see box*), reputedly after being lured to a love nest nearby. His wife, Beatriz de Bobadilla, was notorious throughout Spanish royal circles for her promiscuity. She is said to have entertained Columbus in the tower and rumours speak of an affair. The tower was also used for storing riches from the New World en route to Spain.
Next to the harbour front.

Los Roques

The main southern route from San Sebastián (TF713) passes a number of outstanding volcanic plug rock formations. Most interesting is the **Roque del Sombrero** (8km from town), which resembles a pointed Chinese hat, peaking at 663m. After 16km there is a spectacular, if windy *mirador* at the Degollada (Pass) de Peraza. Looming above it is the mightiest of the rocks, **Roque de Agando** (1,250m). Three notable *roques* on the other side of the road from east to west are: **Carmen** (1,140m), **Zarcita** (1,235m), and **Ojila** (1,169m).

View of San Sebastián from the Parador Nacional

Northern La Gomera

The road to the north of La Gomera is a spectacular winding route calling at the island's most picturesque settlements. If you have just one day on the island, this is the way to go. It also has the advantage of being lower than the southern route, avoiding the clouds that form on the higher ground. Without these, however, there would be no primordial laurisilva forest on La Gomera – a feature much enjoyed by walkers and naturalists.

Garajonay National Park

Agulo

The adjectives 'neat and tidy' best describe this small, pretty village of narrow, cobbled streets. Its position is perfect – enclosed in a natural amphitheatre of rocky cliffs perched high above the sea, with Tenerife's Mount Teide forming a majestic backdrop. In the centre is a curiously designed grey and white painted church with domes showing Moorish influence.

25km northwest of San Sebastián.

Hermigua

Hermigua, the second-largest settlement on the island after San Sebastián, is a long, straggling village clinging to the roadside above a lush valley of banana plantations. Vines are also grown here, strung on bamboo frames which hang diagonally across the hillsides like giant spiders' webs.

Visit the Los Telares craft centre (on the main road) to see the old house where girls still weave on ancient looms. A little further along, stop by the Convento sign. By the side of the plaza is the 16th-century Convento de Santo Domingo, with a fine ceiling and an image of the local saint.

20km northwest of San Sebastián.

Juego de Bolas Centro de Visitantes

This excellent visitor centre should be able to answer most questions you may have about La Gomera. Well-labelled gardens illustrate island flora, a small ethnographical museum covers peasant life, and a complex of workshops demonstrates basketry, weaving, pottery, and woodworking. In the main reception area are displays giving information about the Garajonay National Park.

The road between the visitor centre and the El Tabor bar leads to a newly created *mirador* with spectacular views right down over Agulo and across to Tenerife. The unsurfaced track at the end of the asphalt road may be very bumpy, but is quite short and manageable in an ordinary car.

34km northwest of San Sebastián. Tel: (922) 800993. Open: daily 9.30am–4.30pm.

Parque Nacional de Garajonay (Garajonay National Park)

This 4,000-hectare national park, which is slightly more than 10 per cent of the total area of the island, occupies the island's central high plateau, and owes its protected status to its Canarian laurisilva forest – the largest and most complete known example of the ecosystem left in the world. Laurisilva (a woodland of ferns, laurels, and heath trees) thrives in damp conditions, and much of the forest is cloaked in a veil of mist year-round. In 1986, it was declared a World Heritage Site by UNESCO. During the winter, it is cold and damp, but in summer it dries to such an extent that forest fires are a hazard. The trails within the park are popular with walkers. There are two information centres: at La Laguna Grande (*see p114*) and Juego de Bolas. The highest point on the island, El Alto de Garajonay (Mount Garajonay) at 1,487m, lies within the park, and on a good day it offers excellent views.

Vallehermoso

This compact village hugging the valley side is a fine sight when approached from the TF112 to the north. At the entrance to Vallehermoso is a particularly artistic children's playground. The giant sculpture of three curvaceous ladies with headdresses would grace many a modern art museum. Vallehermoso has a lively centre with two bustling tapas bars, from which old houses rise up to the church.

42km northwest of San Sebastián.

The white houses of Vallehermoso

Walk: Vallehermoso

This walk combines Gomeran landscapes of lush valleys in deep ravines, overlooked by volcanic rocks, with a charming reservoir. It is suitable for any age and fitness level, although the hill is reasonably steep, and much of it could be followed in an ordinary car.

Allow 1–1½ hours.

LA GOMERA
·Vallehermoso
Valle Gran Rey · Hermigua
▲ Garajonay · San
de la
·Playa de Santiago

Start in the centre of Vallehermoso, and follow the road uphill out of town, to the left of the Bar Route Amaya.

1 Roque Cano

The large 'Canine Rock', which protrudes 650m into the sky and dominates the view, is named after its resemblance to a canine tooth. Like so many other volcanic outcrops on the island, it is merely the central volcanic lava plug – the rest of the cone has long been eroded away. As you continue to climb, look back for fine views of

EL SILBO

Compelled by the difficulties imposed by the landscape, the Gomerans have developed a unique language known as el silbo (the whistle). This is no ordinary whistling; it has real modulation, vocabulary, and stentorian volume. It is said that some silbadores can communicate from up to 5km away. With the advent of tele-communications, and the decline of ancient skills, practitioners are becoming rare. The gardener at the parador may well demonstrate silbo for you; otherwise, join the tourist show at Las Rosas restaurant.

The church at Vallehermoso

Vallehermoso and its church. Down to your left, the abundance of the lush valley is clear. Bananas, palm trees, sugar cane, orange groves, and vines all jostle for space.
Continue your climb up the hill, which becomes steeper and rounds a bend.

2 The Valley of 1001 Palms

It is doubtful whether anyone has really counted the trees here, but as many are on tap for Gomera's famous palm-honey (*see p158*), it is possible. Look for metal cups attached to the trunks, catching the 'honey' (palm sap). Metal bands on the trees keep the ants at bay.

Whatever the number of trees, this valley is a splendid sight, particularly in the late afternoon, as the sun shines directly down into it.
After about 20 minutes' walking, you will see the dam wall holding back the reservoir.

3 Embalse de la Encantadora

Despite its function (supplying water to the village and valleys below), this reservoir has a natural, almost ornamental look, hence its romantic name – the Lake of the Enchanted Lady. Ducks bob on its surface, and there is a statue of a man – perhaps a Guanche – stranded on a tiny island with just a pole for company. Walk all the way around the reservoir. You'll probably meet a goat or two en route, tethered and grazing. As you complete the circle, cross the metal bridge, and (if you don't suffer from vertigo) look down the sheer wall of the dam, trickling water into the valley.
Walk back down the hill and take the right turn downhill.

Down here is a very ramshackle smallholding of animals and birds. Don't mind the barking dog (as long as he is attached to his tether!). The path descends all the way to the foot of the dam where there is a small stream. You can cross this to the orange groves on the other side, but you can go no further.
Return to the main road and descend back down into the village.

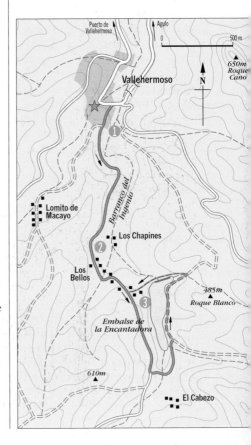

Valle Gran Rey

Southern La Gomera

The south of La Gomera accommodates the island's two tourist resorts, Playa de Santiago, and Valle Gran Rey. Yet both are relatively isolated, and would hardly even register on the average Canarian holiday development scale. The Valle Gran Rey was, until recently, only known by a few hippy-types, whereas the hotel complex at Playa de Santiago attracts a monied clientele.

El Cercado/Chipude
These neighbouring hamlets, divided by a ridge, could almost be twins. Chipude is the more handsome of the pair, enjoying a splendid setting against the foot of the table-top mountain known as La Fortaleza (1,243m).

In El Cercado you can see the craft of *alfareria* – pottery made from the dark Gomeran earth, without a wheel.

El Cercado is 37km northwest of San Sebastián. Chipude is 39km northwest of San Sebastián.

La Laguna Grande
The 'big lagoon' has long gone, but this is a popular meeting point for walkers, as it is an entrance point to the Garajonay National Park (*see p111*). There is an information office and a log cabin, which in winter has a roaring fire. For non-

walkers there is also a children's playground and a barbecue area.
29km northwest of San Sebastián. Open: Tue–Sat 9am–4.30pm. On Fri walking tours depart from here. Reservations are essential. Tel: (922) 800993 (Juego de Bolas office).

Playa de Santiago
The stony beach here is in the infancy of development, with a handful of bars and restaurants lining its new promenade. At the far end is a small fishing port. Above the beach, the Hotel Jardín Tecina is very much in the vanguard of Gomeran tourism. With over 400 rooms, this is a veritable giant, but it has not abused its power. The architecture is vernacular, and rooms are in village-style bungalows, set in beautifully laid out

LOS ORGANOS

Los Organos (the organ pipes) is an extraordinary 200m-wide formation of slender, tightly-packed basalt columns. Some of these reach over 80m high and they do, indeed, resemble giant petrified church organ pipes.

Los Organos is located just off the north coast and may only be viewed from the sea. Boats depart from Valle de Gran Rey, Playa de Santiago and San Sebastián. For further details contact the Tourist Information office in San Sebastián.

grounds. Excursions and walking tours may be organised here through the Gomera Safari travel agency. Notice the colourful statues outside the hotel. The grinning conquistador is understandably pleased with himself, but the native figure (presumably meant to be a Guanche) looks as if he would be far more at home in North America.
34km southwest of San Sebastián. Tourist office: Edificio Las Vistas, 8, Avenida Maritima. Tel: (922) 895650.

Valle Gran Rey

The origin of the name 'Valley of the Great King' goes back to Guanche times, but this is still a place fit for royalty. There is only one road into the valley, and it is arguably the most beautiful on the island. Towards the bottom the views to the emerald green slopes on the far side are breathtaking, with row upon row of little white houses perched precariously on steep terraces.

At the valley bottom, the road splits – left goes to the port, and right goes to La Playa Calera. The latter is the only sandy beach on the island, and is showing signs of small-scale development. The pretty village of La Calera lies behind the resort.

En route to the Valle Gran Rey, stop at the Mirador del Santo at Arure (10km north of La Calera). It is one of the finest viewpoints on the island.
Valle Gran Rey is 52km west of San Sebastián. Tourist office: Calle Lepanto. Tel: (922) 805458.

Cultivated terraces at the top of the Valle Gran Rey

La Palma

La Palma is quite unlike the other, smaller Canary Islands, and in many ways stands superior to its larger cousins. It is known throughout the Canaries as La Isla Verde (the Green Island), due to its comparative abundance of water. For the farmers this means profitable banana, tobacco, and avocado crops; for tourists it means the most tropical and, many would argue, the most beautiful landscape in the archipelago. This natural beauty is enhanced by the islanders' homes and gardens, which are often said to be the best kept in the Canaries.

Hiking in the Caldera de Taburiente

La Palma has a relatively prosperous history. Its capital, Santa Cruz de la Palma, was one of only three Spanish ports allowed to trade with the Americas for a period in the 16th century, and even today, its aristocratic past is visible.

Rolling clouds at El Paso

The island doesn't excel in beach holidays. With just a few black beaches and its isolation from the major islands, it attracts only a handful of tourists in search of peace and natural beauty. Their main aim is the Caldera de Taburiente – a massive crater formed some 400,000 years ago by an earth-shattering explosion, subsequently smoothed and greened by nature into an outstanding beauty spot now enjoying Spanish national park status. By contrast, the most recent volcanic activity in the Canaries also happened on the island, in 1971. You can still feel the heat beneath your feet.

Two more features help explain the island's dramatic natural appeal. In relation to its surface area it lays claim to be the tallest island in the world. If you reach the summit (at 2,426m), you will see a gleaming set of domes housing international telescopes, for La Palma also boasts the clearest, darkest sky in the northern hemisphere.

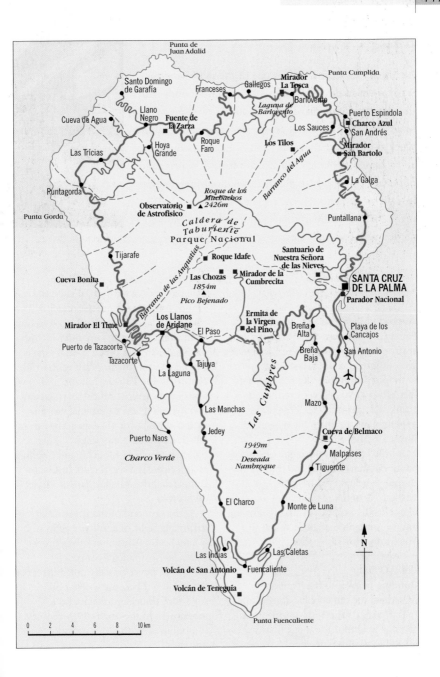

Santa Cruz

Architecturally, Santa Cruz is one of the most handsome small towns in the archipelago. Its wealth from trade with the Americas may have passed, but its well-preserved buildings reflect a sense of prosperity. Tourism has hardly touched the town. There are two low-key museums here, and a *parador*, although you could walk past the latter and not even know it existed. But the town has plenty to offer in terms of authentic Spanish colonial atmosphere, and by night, the Avenida Marítima becomes a lively promenade of pavement bars and cafés.

Avenida Marítima

Tourist information office: Avenida Marítima, 34. Tel: (922) 423340.

Avenida Marítima

Santa Cruz has one of the least spoiled seafronts of any town in the Canaries. At its southern end is a bizarre dragon tree with four 'heads' peering out on long 'necks', set at 90 degrees to the main trunk. The parador (*see p164*) is an appetiser for the splendid, balconied houses further along.

A little further along is the Castillo de Santa Catalina, built in the 16th century, though much altered in later years. Its entrance is to the rear, but it is presently closed to the public. For hiking, touring and camping information, ask at the Tourist Information office.

Calle O'Daly

Running parallel to the Avenida Marítima, the old cobbled street Calle O'Daly reflects the 17th- and 18th-century wealth of the town, boasting several handsome merchants' houses.

The street is named after an Irish banana merchant who settled on the island (towards the northern end it changes its name to Calle Real). Walking from south to north, look out for Nos. 42, 38, 28, 26 and 24. Of special note is No. 22, built in the first half of the 17th century as the **Palacio Salazar**, and now housing the tourist office. After passing through the Plaza de España, visit the casino at No. 7 (or 15, depending on which numbering you follow). This building, a mix of Moorish and Colonial architecture, is a social club. Just below is the delightful small square of Placeta de Borreo.

At the very end of the street is the surprising sight of a full-size galleon. It is a replica of Columbus's flagship, the *Santa María*, made of concrete. Columbus never actually called here, but the island did become wealthy on American trade, and this is also a monument to the town's 19th-century shipbuilders. Within it is a small naval museum.

Plaza de la Alameda. Tel: (922) 416550. Open: Mon–Thur 9.30am–2pm, 4–7pm, Fri 9.30am–2pm. Admission charge.

Plaza de España

This fine ensemble of historic buildings is the heart of the capital. Look inside the 16th-century **Iglesia del Salvador** (Church of the Saviour). The ceiling is a splendid example of *mudéjar (see p81)* woodwork, and its Gothic arched sacristy is also notable. Its treasures include a painted altarpiece, and a remarkable silver cross in a rear chapel. Adjacent to the church is a fine drinking fountain. The beautiful building on the corner of the plaza now houses the well-known Spanish Open University.

The ***ayuntamiento*** (town hall) was built in 1569 with a Renaissance arcade and a fine colonial interior; it was once the Cardinal's palace. Step inside during office hours to admire the colourful mural by Mariano de Cossío on the stairway, and the outstanding carved panelling ceiling.

Take care on the cobbles of Calle O'Daly

Northern La Palma

San Andrés aside, the northern villages of La Palma are unexceptional, and a tour of the whole northern loop can be a tiring experience. However, if the weather is clear, it is worth making the journey to the Roque de los Muchachos, which passes some of the island's most dramatic scenery, and ends in spectacular style, peering into the depths of Caldera de Taburiente.

Los Tilos

Los Tilos (the lime trees) is a damp ancient laurisilva forest of limes, laurels, myrtles, and ferns. Water flows so thick and fast here, down the Barranco del Agua, that a hydroelectric plant (the only one in the Canary Islands) has been constructed. There is a picnic area, and a visitor centre is planned.
29.5km north of Santa Cruz.

Parve Laguna de Barlovento

Just a few kilometres south of Barlovento, this lovely park has a charming lake with panoramic views of the countryside around.
Tourist office: Tel: (922) 696023.

Puntagorda

On the northwest of the island, this sparsely inhabited, straggling agricultural settlement lacks any real centre. However, the flower and vegetable fields around here are pretty, particularly in spring, when the pink almond trees bloom.
28km north of Los Llanos de Aridane.

Roque de los Muchachos

At 2,426m, this is the highest point on the island, perched on the edge of the Caldera de Taburiente (*see pp124–5*).

The road which leads here is tortuous, scenic (lunar-like in places), and passes through clouds before bursting back into sunlight near the top.

This peak is always cold, and in winter is often covered in snow (in very bad weather the road is cut off). Having braved the journey, there are breathtaking views down into the *caldera* (crater),

NORTHERN MIRADORES

There are two fine *miradores* to look out for while touring the north. Just north of La Galga (19km north of Santa Cruz), look for the signpost Mirador La Montaña. Stop by the small church of Ermita de San Bartolomé for a view along the east coast, then drive uphill to the Mirador San Bartolo, which has panoramic views inland.

At the very top of the island, just west of Barlovento, turn right towards Gallegos. After just over 1km the Mirador La Tosca gives views along the north coast. Look down to your right to a curious colony of dragon trees (*see p42*).

and nearby are the intriguing white and silver domes of the Observatorio de Astrofísico (Astrophysical Observatory), which opened in 1985 (*see pp122–3*).
44km northwest of Santa Cruz.

San Andrés y los Sauces

Set on the northeast coast, the top half of this twinned village, Los Sauces, is a modern agricultural centre of little interest. But take the road down through the dense banana plantations to San Andrés, and you will find a charming square shared by a 17th-century church, well-tended gardens, and a popular fish restaurant. From here old houses tumble down the steep cobbled hill towards the sea.

Near San Andrés is Charco Azul (the Blue Pool), a pleasantly situated semi-natural lido with refreshments.
San Andrés is 28km north of Santa Cruz.

Santuario de Nuestra Señora de las Nieves (Sanctuary of Our Lady of the Snows)

The village of Las Nieves is the most sacred spot on the island, though curiously 'the snows' refer not to the island peaks, but to a 4th-century miracle, when the Virgin appeared during an unusual snowfall in August in Rome.

The focus of attention is the 14th-century terracotta figure of the Virgin, the island's patron saint, and probably the oldest image in all the islands. There is some fine gold- and silver-work in the 17th-century chapel which houses the figure, and a restaurant in the square. Every five years (in August) the figure is brought down to Santa Cruz in a grand procession known as La Bajada de la Virgen (the descent of the Virgin). Great festivities follow. The next *bajada* is in the year 2010.
3½km west of Santa Cruz.

The tree line at the Caldera de Taburiente

La Palma Observatory

Why on earth is one of the most important observatories in the northern hemisphere sited on an obscure Canary Island? The answer is that La Palma provides a combination of geographical, topographical and meteorological factors which is perfect for star-gazing.

The remoteness of the island and its lack of development means that the observatory (El Observatorio del Roque de los Muchachos), is free from distracting artificial light; the shape of the mountain and the prevailing winds mean the airflow here is comparatively undisturbed; and the site is above the clouds (which trap dust and moisture) for the vast majority of the year. Put all these together, and it means that

extremely faint stars and galaxies, mind-boggling distances away, can be observed with the utmost clarity.

The observatory complex was inaugurated in 1985, and is host to a number of different international organisations. The largest observatory is operated by the Isaac Newton Group of Telescopes (*www.ing.iac.es*) and includes the William Herschel telescope. This is the largest in Europe and, with the advantage of its La Palma site and the quality of its instrumentation, it is one of the finest windows on the universe in the world.

If you would like to see inside, the observatory is open only three times a year, in summer (*Tel: (922) 405500, www.iac.es/orm/visitas/indice.htm*).

Don't expect to look through a working telescope, however. 'Telescope time' here is fought over by professional astronomers from all over the world, and is usually three times over-subscribed.

Disappointingly for romantics, the popular image of the astronomer with his eye to the lens, wrapped in scarves to keep warm, is well out of date. Eyes are rarely put to lenses on La Palma, and the telescopes are remote-controlled from computer consoles, while operators sit in warm, comfortable rooms.

Views of the observatory above the clouds

View of the *caldera* crater

Southern La Palma

This southern loop of La Palma includes the most picturesque villages and, from Fuencaliente to Los Llanos de Aridane, the most scenic driving stretch of the island. Pine forests sweep down the hillside to pretty roadside hamlets, while superb coastal views open out ahead. The mountains loom ever closer and the Mirador de la Cumbrecita, the climax of the drive, provides unforgettable views into the Caldera de Taburiente.

Fuencaliente

This neat village is famous for its two volcanoes and its wine, both of which can easily be sampled by taking a walk around the volcanoes (*see pp126–7*), then visiting the bodegas (wine cellars).
33km south of Santa Cruz.
Bodegas de Teneguía. Tel: (922) 454545. Open: Mon–Fri 9am–2pm & 3–5pm (winter), 8am–1pm (summer).

Los Llanos de Aridane

It is easy to drive along the dual carriageway that bypasses Los Llanos and completely miss the old centre of town. Instead, turn right here (heading from Santa Cruz), and you will find a charming plaza with an early 16th-century church, **Iglesia de los Remedios**, a typically Canarian *ayuntamiento* (town hall), and café tables and chairs spreading beneath ancient Indian laurel trees. Step behind the church, and there are more fine old houses, and a view of the mountains. Nearby, the Mirador El Time offers spectacular views back along the south coast from an almost sheer elevation of 594m.
32km west of Santa Cruz.

Mazo

Saturday afternoon and Sunday morning markets bring tourists and locals to this small village. Do look into the fine 16th-century Iglesia de San Blás which has a number of 16th-century statues, and a fine high altar. Just outside the village on the road to Hoya de Mazo is the highly-regarded pottery workshop of El Molino.
Some 4km south of Mazo, Guanche inscriptions may be found in the Cueva (Cave) de Belmaco.
Mazo is 15km south of Santa Cruz.

Parque Nacional de la Caldera de Taburiente (National Park of the Crater of Taburiente)

The protected area of the *caldera*, or crater, measures 9km across at its widest point and has a circumference of 28km. It was formed some 400,000 years ago in a massive explosion, and since then the elements have gouged the crater even deeper (down to 900m), and have turned it into one of the most green and beautiful places in the archipelago.

There is only one surfaced road into the national park, and that is from the south, leading to the spectacular Mirador de la Cumbrecita. There is an information kiosk here, from where free guided walks start (pre-booking essential). There are more views from Lomo de Las Chozas, 1km due west. Serious walkers also enter the park from its southwest corner via the Barranco de las Angustias. This *barranco* (ravine) was the last bastion of La Palma's Guanches, and the great monolith known as Roque Idafe was a sacred point to them.

Mirador de la Cumbrecita is 30km west of Santa Cruz. Tel: (922) 497277.

Tazacorte

The upper part of Tazacorte retains much of its old character, and is pleasantly laid out, with a promenade looking over dense green banana plantations down towards Puerto de Tazacorte. The focal point is a raised plaza where the locals sit under a bougainvillea-decked pergola next to a pretty church.

The fishing port of Puerto de Tazacorte, 3km to the north, has a black sand beach served by a handful of bars and restaurants.

The west coast's largest resort is Puerto Naos, 11km south of Tazacorte. This has a much larger beach, and on it the 300-bed, 4-star Sol Élite – by far the biggest and most luxurious hotel on the island (*see p169*).

Tazacorte is 38km west of Santa Cruz.

Trekking along the edge of the *caldera*

Walk: La Palma Volcanoes

This walk shows you two of La Palma's volcanoes (one still warm!) in a spectacular coastal setting. The walk around Volcán de San Antonio is a level 30-minute circle, open to everyone, although it does become slightly vertiginous on the far side. The walk down to Volcán de Teneguía is rather steep, but you have the option of driving down to it. The walk up to the rim of Volcán de Teneguía is short but strenuous, and should not be attempted in windy weather. *Allow 1½ to 2 hours total walking time if you descend all the way from the village of Fuencaliente to Volcán de Teneguía – arrange in the Bar Parada in Fuencaliente for a taxi to collect you at the bottom.*

To get to the Volcán de San Antonio, look out for the small sign on the main road in the middle of Fuencaliente opposite the Bar Parada. It is a ten-minute walk or a two-minute drive to the crater car park. Follow the directional arrow that leads you anti-clockwise around the rim of the volcano.*

Low cloud fills the volcano's crater

1 Volcán de San Antonio

This 657-m high volcano erupted over the course of 66 days in 1667 and is now starting to look mature, with pine trees on its lower inner slopes and foliage higher up.

To your right, sloping down towards the sea, is the village of Las Indias. As you round the edge of the volcano there are excellent views back to the village of Fuencaliente (*see p124*), framed by evergreen hills. The volcano drops away steeply to the sea, and below are wonderful views of Volcán de Teneguía. On a sunny day the volcano reveals its shades of browns, reds, and purples, but even when plain matt-black, it is a colourful sight against the clear blue Atlantic Ocean.

If you visit in summer, the space between the two volcanoes is covered in leafy vines, bright lime-green against the black lava-fields. The farmers of Fuencaliente have taken advantage of the natural disaster to cultivate some of the most unusual vines which thrive on this soil.

Just before you complete the circle around the rim, a path drops away to your right. Follow this, then follow the winding paths that snake downhill to Teneguía, which is clearly visible. Head for the car park. Alternatively, if you want a shorter walk, return to your car, continue driving downhill, and take the sharp left turn towards Los Quemados. Take the track signposted 'Teneguía 1971', then take the first turning right, which takes you down to the car park. The ascent to the rim of the volcano takes 20–30 minutes.

2 Volcán de Teneguía

This is the youngest volcano in the archipelago, having erupted for 25 days as recently as 1971. It is said that the fountain of lava cascaded 200m into the air, and it produced the equivalent of two million lorry-loads of lava, but no one was hurt. Lava-streams spread down to the coast, towards the lighthouse and saltpans, and have actually extended the island by a few metres. Hot gases still emanate through the crater walls, and the ground is warm. Don't worry, the volcano is receding.

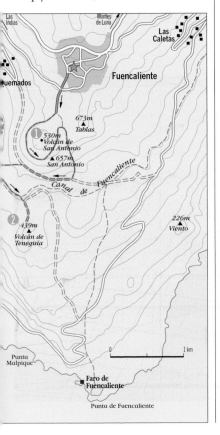

El Hierro

El Hierro is the most westerly, the smallest, and the least known of all the Canary Islands. As if to underline the point, Las Puntas is the home of what is claimed to be the world's smallest hotel. Such solitude and lack of pretensions inevitably draw a small following of visitors who come here for the walking, and peace and quiet which is offered by the island.

El Golfo

A huge crater runs down to the sea on El Hierro

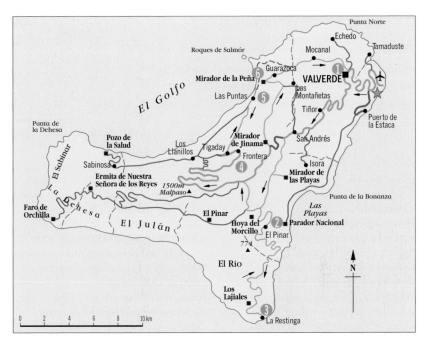

The history of the island is also fairly uneventful. The Herreños were the only Canarians to surrender peaceably to the Spanish invaders. Unfortunately, they did not foresee that the conquistadores would then sell them into slavery. According to a popular belief, in 1493, Columbus may have called here during his second voyage to the New World.

The great natural feature of El Hierro is the bay of El Golfo (the Gulf). This is thought to be the rim of a massive crater, half of which is submerged, and half of which rises dramatically to over 1,000m. El Hierro has other natural scenery to rival the best in the Canaries: splendid pine forests; strange, twisted juniper trees unique to the island; sheer mountain walls; and spectacular *miradores*.

There is however a shortage of accommodation. The *parador* would seem the most comfortable choice, but it is isolated even by El Hierro standards. If you intend staying overnight, book ahead (*see pp163–4*).

Touring can be frustrating. El Hierro may only be 24km by 27km at its maximum dimensions, but the configuration of its roads means that a good deal of backtracking is inevitable. The west of the island can only be explored along slow and bumpy dirt tracks, and the south coast is all but inaccessible.

Tourist information office: Calle del Dr. Quintero, 4. Tel: (922) 550302.
Open: Mon–Fri 8.30am–2.30pm,
Sat 9am–1pm.

Drive: El Hierro

This tour is designed for visitors with just one day on the island, and takes in virtually all the island highlights. For the route, see the El Hierro map on page 129.

Allow 5–6 hours.

From the airport follow the winding road inland for 7km.

1 Valverde

The island capital's only sign of importance is the sturdy late-18th-century church, **Iglesia de la Concepción**, that once gave protection against corsairs. Aside from a small ornamental plaza and a tourist office, it is essentially just a village. In the centre of Valverde there is the **Casa de las Quinteras,** a museum of the island's way of life displaying agricultural and tradesmen's tools, domestic implements, folk costumes and local arts and crafts.

(Calle Armas Martel. Open: Mon–Fri 8.30am–2.30pm. Admission charge.)
Head south through San Andrés and turn left towards El Pinar.

2 El Pinar

Gently rolling countryside of beautiful pine forests makes up this area with the small settlement of the same name at its heart.

Stop at the Mirador de las Playas for a wonderful view of the bay of Las Playas. The building with the red-tiled roof is the island *parador.*
Continue south for 13km.

3 La Restinga

This fishing port is marked by an ugly seawall which does at least create calm swimming conditions. Adventurous German tourists are cultivating La Restinga into something of a frontier resort. As you head along this road, note the strange rope-lava landscape just north of La Restinga.

Return to El Pinar and turn off left onto the secondary road towards Frontera. Turn left again as the road rejoins the main one.

4 Frontera

As the road descends to the coast, fine views of El Golfo appear. Tantalising views also appear of the church of Frontera. From afar it seems tiny and hopelessly isolated against the great green-grey mountain wall that makes up one side of El Golfo. But on closer inspection, this is just a small bell tower built on a volcanic cone – the church itself is on the road below.

Frontera is the island's wine-growing centre, and interested tourists may like to visit the large, deserted antique *lagares* (winepresses) occasionally seen on the hillsides.

Continue on the TF912 to Tigaday; turn right to head downhill towards the sea.

5 Las Puntas

Aside from the 'world's smallest hotel' by the remains of the old harbour, there's not much at Las Puntas, but it's a pleasant drive down to the sea with its rocky outcrops. Almost directly above to the right is the Mirador de la Peña.
Backtrack all the way beyond Frontera, and after 20km turn left onto a minor road to the Mirador de Jinama. Continue, and turn left onto the main road.

6 Mirador de la Peña

This superb, enclosed viewing point is the work of César Manrique. The cliff on which it is perched falls almost a sheer 600m to the sea, offering the best view of El Golfo on the island. Note the strange native *sabina* (juniper) tree outside the *mirador*, grotesquely twisted by the fierce winds, yet still alive. A small forest of these exists at El Sabinar in the west of the island.
Return 8km east to Valverde and turn left to the airport.

Tourist information office: Calle del Licenciado Bueno 1. *Tel: (922) 550302.* Open: Mon–Sat 8.30am–2.30pm.
Valverde museums Both have unpredictable opening times; enquire at the tourist information office.

The twisted *sabina* tree at Mirador de la Peña

The Canary Islands are proud of their continuous sunshine but they could just as easily boast about another climatic resource, strong and healthy winds. The islands would not look as they do were it not for the trade winds generated by the Azores anticyclone which keep temperatures from soaring and deliver plentiful precipitation for the growth of thick subtropical vegetation.

To windsurfers, of course, the combination of sun and wind is ideal and they take full advantage, most famously at El Médano, on the east coast of Tenerife but also at Playa de las Américas, Tenerife, and on Gran Canaria at Maspalomas, Pozo Izquierdo, and Playa de Vargas.

More significantly, perhaps, the same force that drives the windsurfers is being increasingly harnessed to turn the blades of modern wind turbines (don't call them windmills) to generate pollution-free 'renewable' electricity. The trade winds can blow at up to 8 or 10 metres a second and are consistent enough in places to make wind energy a viable proposition. The two biggest windfarms in Tenerife are both visible from the east-coast motorway. They are at Granadilla near El Médano and a little north of there at Finca de Mogán in Arico. On Gran Canaria, Juan Grande windfarm, due south of Vecindario, is also within sight of the motorway and there is a single conspicuous turbine beside the airport.

The Canary Islands' wind power capacity may still be modest but it is growing and is part of a sizeable industry. Spain is the world's second biggest generator of wind power in the world, after Germany.

From afar a wind turbine looks sleek and fragile, but get up close and the scale of the thing becomes apparent. A typical turbine tower will be anything over 30 metres high – the equivalent of a 7-storey building – often much higher. The wind drives the three twisted blades around in a circle with a diameter of about 45 metres – roughly half the length of a soccer pitch – and shafts and gears carry the force to the generator where electricity is produced. If the wind blows too strongly, an automatic brake stops the blades before they buckle or snap.

Wind power tends to raise strong reactions in people, either for or against it. While some people praise the (albeit small) contribution it makes towards slowing climate change, others complain that wind turbines are unsightly. Two specific objections to them, however – that they are noisy and a danger to birds – have not been borne out by studies. You can usually only hear the noise of the swishing blades when you are close to the turbines and statistically more birds are killed by cars than wind turbine blades.

Wind power has proven itself to be the first commercially-viable form of renewable electricity, and the technology is improving in efficiency all the time with corresponding reductions in costs. The smallest Canary Island, El Hierro, a designated UNESCO biosphere reserve, wants to take the green philosophy to its limit and become the first island in the world to be 100 per cent powered by renewable energy, using a mixture of wind and hydro-electric power.

Wind turbines near Agaete, Gran Canaria

Beyond the Resorts

Getting away from it all need never present a problem in the Canary Islands. This is self-evident for those travelling to the quiet islands of El Hierro, La Palma, and La Gomera, but even on the major resort islands it is true. The very fact that mega-resorts have been built on the south coasts of Tenerife and Gran Canaria means that tourism is contained within well-defined limits.

Valle Gran Rey

Adventure Excursions
Jeep Safaris
If you want to get off the main roads and see the landscape, you might consider joining a jeep safari. The best of these explore tracks which most drivers of hired cars fear (or are simply unable) to tread. There are drawbacks, however. The back of a jeep is hard, cramped and particularly uncomfortable in inclement weather. Even in mildly hot weather, you run the risk of returning badly sunburned and very dehydrated. Many people are known to have spent the following days in bed! It is also impossible for a tour leader to give a running commentary. Some jeep safaris let their clients drive. If you want to try your four-wheel drive skills this may be fine, but you may not be so happy being driven at high speeds over rough ground by a novice whom you have never met before! Jeep excursions are available on all the islands (except El Hierro) through a number of operators, and are widely advertised.

Boat Safaris
Boat trips (or 'safaris') are widely available from most of the larger tourist resorts, and can be a good way to see a different aspect of an island. However, you should always find out what you are letting yourself in for in advance. Do you really want 'free' wine and 'pirate games', or would you prefer coastal views and undisturbed relaxation?

A bewildering variety of craft is available – sailing yachts, large motor launches, small motor launches, glass-hulled catamarans, and the antique *Nostramo*, built in 1918. If you would prefer to skipper your own course, it's easy to charter a boat from pleasure marinas or yacht clubs (*club náuticos*). (*See p151.*)

The ports of southern Gran Canaria offer the most varied choice of boat excursions (*see pp56–57*) but the most interesting boat safaris depart from southern Tenerife in search of dolphins and whales off the southwest coast. Some 200 short-finned pilot whales live and breed just offshore, and these can normally be seen together with bottle-nosed dolphins.

TENERIFE
Nostramo
Daily sailings from Playa San Juan to

Los Gigantes cliffs. Five-hour cruise with lunch and the possibility of seeing whales and dolphins. The company has two other boats fitted with live underwater television cameras.
Ocean Center, 15, Costa Adeje. Tel: (922) 750085.

Lady Shelley
Glass-bottomed catamaran offering daily excursions in search of whales and dolphins.
Office in Pirámide de Arona (Mare Nostrum resort), Playa de las Américas. Tel: (922) 757549.

Horse Riding
This is a near-perfect way to get off the beaten track, with excursions both through inland countryside and along deserted beaches. There are several riding stables which offer tuition (even for complete beginners) and accompanied rides.

GRAN CANARIA
Bandama Golf Club Riding School
Tel: (928) 351290.

Maspalomas Oasis Riding School
Tel: (928) 772404.

El Salobre Riding School
Off the Palmitos Park road towards Tablero.
Tel: (928) 140378.

Real Club de Golf
Santa Brigida Tel: (928) 354991.

Rancho Grande
Moonlit rides and pony rides for children.
Juan Grande Tel: (928) 728115.

Boats in the harbour at Los Cristianos

The beach at Puerto de Mogán is always popular

TENERIFE
Los Brezos
Riding lessons and treks led by certified instructors.
Camino Candelaria, Monte, 101, Tacoronte. Tel: (922) 567222.

Mamio Verde
Accompanied rides through the hills of La Orotava, Santa Ursula and La Victoria.
Cuadras de Pino Alto, 39, La Orotava. Tel: (922) 333956.

El Molino
Riding lessons and rides in the local countryside.
*Lomo las Rias, carretera general del Socorro, Tegueste.
Tel: (922) 541658.*

Rancho Grande Amarilla Golf & Country Club
Lessons for beginners and children. Accompanied rides in the countryside.
Urbanización Amarilla Golf, San Miguel de Abona. Tel: (922) 730319.

Beaches
Conventional wisdom suggests that you need a four-wheel drive vehicle to find the away-from-it-all beaches. However, this is not always the case. One of the finest beaches in all the islands, Playa de las Teresitas at Santa Cruz on the main coast road of Tenerife, is quiet for most of the year. If you find yourself on a solitary beach, particularly one facing north or west (this applies to all the islands), swim with great caution, if at all. Currents can be treacherous, and a number of holidaymakers seeking solitude have come to grief.

Naturalists can take cover among the dunes at Maspalomas on Gran Canaria, or at Las Gaviotas, next to Playa de las Teresitas, on Tenerife.

Cycling

Bikes are available for hire at most major resorts and there are several companies offering guided mountain bike excursions with lunch included. The climate certainly suits cycling and a bicycle can be an excellent way of getting about a resort; but the hilly terrain inland is not to everyone's taste and you probably won't want to attempt a mountainous route unless you are feeling particularly fit.

Walking

Whilst a hire car is certainly the best way to get an overall impression of the islands if you haven't much time, roads don't reach everywhere and you won't really get to know the countryside of the Canary Islands at all unless you are prepared to walk. A hike across hillsides of wildflowers alive with birdsong, away from the busy beaches and shopping centres of the resorts can be the perfect way to unwind. At first sight, the islands may not look all that tempting to the casual walker as there is a steep slope in almost every direction and few footpaths are waymarked. But if there are hills there are also great views at every turn and as soon as you gain a little altitude the climate becomes more conducive to hill walking – sunny but not too hot. The good news is that signposting is improving all the time as the authorities try to lure tourists away from the coasts and into the interior, and

there are ever more good restaurants and bars where you can punctuate a vigorous day's exercise.

As a general rule, the best walking is to be found in the north and centre of the islands; the south is usually too hot and too dry. Tenerife leads the way in signposting walks, and a favourite, easy route is the Barranco del Infierno at Adeje (*see p104*). Gran Canaria is doing well in renovating the network of paths, or *caminos reales*, that served the island until the first roads were built at the end of the 19th century. There are 1,500km of such paths criss-crossing the island, converging on the Cruz de Tejeda (*see p48*) and over 300km of them have been restored as hiking trails.

Various walking maps and guide books in English are available in bookshops on the islands. The Gran

You need to be fit to take on the mountainous terrain

Canaria tourist government publishes its own guidebook in English, *Mountain Walks on Gran Canaria*, as well as leaflets and maps in Spanish.

If you are going out walking anywhere, the usual advice applies; just because you are on holiday don't take unnecessary chances. You'll need stout walking shoes (boots are best) for walks of any length, plus water, sunhat and warm clothing if you are walking at high altitudes. Never walk alone, and always tell someone when you expect to be back.

Walking Tours

Surprisingly, there are very few commercial walking tour operators on the islands but the national park authorities run free guided walks – all you need to do is phone the relevant visitors' centre to reserve a place. For Tenerife's Mount Teide (*see pp96–9*), for Garajonay on La Gomera (*p111*), and Caldera de Taburiente on La Palma (*pp124–5*). These visitor centres also supply maps and details of marked walks you can do on your own.

GRAN CANARIA
Finca Britannica
Experienced British walking guides based in southern Gran Canaria.
Fataga. Tel: (928) 798150.

TENERIFE
Senderos Turísticos Gregorio
Tenerife's leading walking tour company collects from various points in Puerto de la Cruz. Trips include an ascent of Teide from 2,300 metres, a path through the Anaga mountains and an excursion to

Join a hike to the Roques de García

the cliffs of Los Gigantes, partly on foot and partly by boat.
Tel: (639) 332761.

LA GOMERA
Timah
Hikes departing from Valle de Gran Rey or from Hotel Tecina.
Valle de Gran Rey. Tel: (900) 101108.

Botany and Bird Watching

The pleasures of walking in the Canary Islands countryside are much increased if you know something about the wildlife to be seen on the way. Fortunately there are a number of nature guides available in English. The standard work on plants native to the islands is *Wild Flowers of the Canary Islands* by David and Zoe Bramwell. For bird watching you want Tony Clarke and David Collins' *A Birdwatchers' Guide to the Canary Islands*.

Walkers in the Llano de Ucanca

Shopping

The first lesson to learn when shopping in the Canaries is to take all those 'tax-free' and 'duty-free' signs with a pinch of salt. The islands were declared a duty-free zone in 1852 by the Spanish authorities in order to stimulate trade, and ever since then they have retained certain privileges (they are now in fact a 'trade-free' zone, which means they are free of certain import taxes), but these benefits are not necessarily all passed on to the customer.

Old shop sign, Tenerife

The luxury goods on which favourable tax rates apply are typically electrical items, cameras, calculators, jewellery, perfume, leather goods and tobacco and spirits. The last two items are certainly bargains, but elsewhere there is often little to choose between Canarian retailers and international airport duty-free shop prices.

Island Goods

There is no doubt that the most satisfying purchases are of those traditional wares made on the islands, sometimes right before your eyes: basketry, woodcarvings, pottery, rugs, and embroidered tableware. You will find *centros de artesanía* (craft workshops) throughout the islands but, despite their often rustic nature, their wares are not always cheap. This is because many hours' labour go into them (unlike the machine-produced Far East imports you will see sold on the streets, and in some shops).

Canarian consumables which make interesting presents or tasty souvenirs include *mojo* sauces (*see p157*) in small gift packs, and wines you can sample in the bodegas of La Palma. Cigars are also a speciality of La Palma, with large Havana-style torpedoes in foil and wooden boxes, making eye-catching and high-quality presents. These compare very favourably with the best Cuban cigars.

A bunch of *strelitzias* (*see pp42–3*) is an exotic way of saying it with flowers. Florists will box these for you so that they may go straight into the aircraft hold (or you can buy them from street sellers, unboxed, at half the price). *Strelitzias* are hardy travellers and will last for a good number of weeks once cut. Dragon tree seeds are available at some gift shops. But note that the Ministry of Agriculture at home may impose certain restrictions on importing plants.

Markets

The most colourful shopping in the Canaries takes place on a Sunday morning. Each of the two provincial capitals of Santa Cruz (Tenerife) and Las Palmas (Gran Canaria) stages a bustling *rastro* (flea market) with a strong African influence. Eclectic is the only way to describe the range of goods on offer at these jamborees. The event, which is something of a carnival, is as important as the merchandise.

The best daily markets are also held in the capitals. Nuestra Señora de Africa, at Santa Cruz de Tenerife, is an attraction in its own right, while the market hall in the Triana area of Las Palmas is the oldest in the Canaries. Gran Canaria also stages notable Sunday markets at San Mateo and Teror.

Other popular markets include the Mercadillo La Havana in La Orotava, Tenerife (on the terrace above the bus station) on Saturdays (9am–3pm), which sells antiques, crafts, and leather goods.

Ask at the tourist office for details of local market days, particularly if you are self-catering.

Shops

Normal shop opening hours are Monday to Saturday 9am or 10am to 1pm or 2pm, and 4pm or 5pm to 7pm or 8pm. In resorts, some shops and supermarkets may stay open all day. All the shops listed below are open during these times unless otherwise stated.

Where to Buy
GRAN CANARIA

Las Palmas is the 'duty-free' mecca of the Canaries. If you can't find the camera you want at a competitive price in the maze of shops between Santa Catalina Parque and the beach, you probably won't find it anywhere. For a classier range of shops, including branches of two of Spain's best

Traditional-style shop in Santa Cruz

Model fishing boats make a good gift

department stores, look on the Avenida de Mesa y López. At the other end of town, more department stores and antique shops can be found on Calle Mayor Triana.

The south is well supplied with shops. The resorts have many ugly *centros commerciales* (shopping centres), where some good bargains and tourist memorabilia can be found.

TENERIFE

Santa Cruz rivals Las Palmas for its 'duty-free' goods, and the shops in the traffic-free central area of Plaza de la Candelaria, Béthencourt Alfonso, and Calle del Castillo are very popular.

Puerto de la Cruz has interesting shops in its centre, and neighbouring La Orotava combines shopping with sightseeing and craft heritage centres.

Shopping opportunities in the south of the island are generally poor.

LA GOMERA/LA PALMA/EL HIERRO

There are few shops on these islands. Look for local wines and liqueurs, palm-honey (*see p158*), Guanche-style pottery, and handicrafts.

What to Buy
GRAN CANARIA
Galeria de Arte, Fataga
Unusual local pottery and good paintings.
Calle Diaz, 8.
Tel: (928) 798123.

El Corte Inglés, Las Palmas
The doyen of Spanish department stores; everything from cheap electrical goods to exclusive designer clothes.
Avenida José Mesa y López, 18.
Tel: (928) 263000.
Open: all day Mon–Sat.

Tienda de Playa del Inglés, Playa del Inglés
A craft initiative featuring the work of potters, woodworkers, and other artisans.
In the tourist office on Avenida de Estados Unidos.

Tel: (928) 772445.
Open: Mon–Fri.

LA PALMA

Island craftwork is on sale in the tourist information offices at:
Plaza de San Francisco, Santa Cruz de La Palma Tel: (922) 412129.
Casa Massieu Vandale, Llano de Argual, 31, Los Llanos de Aridane. Tel: (922) 428455.
Doctor Morera, Villa de Mazo, Tel: (922) 401899.

TENERIFE
El Corte Inglés, Santa Cruz

The nationwide department store has two branches in Tenerife.
Calle El Pilar, 3. Tel: (922) 849444, and Avenida Tres de Mayo, 7. Tel: (922) 849400. Open all day Mon–Sat.

Casa del Vino Canario

A delicatessen selling cheeses, wines, gofio products and other good things to eat from Tenerife.
Plaza de la Pila, 4, Icod de los Vinos. Tel: (922) 813311.

La Casa de los Balcones, La Orotava

Spectacular historic building (*see p84*)

with a large range of craft and souvenir items – embroidery a speciality. The Casa del Turista opposite is under the same management. The same company has outlets at Garachico (Centro El Limonero *see p94*), Puerto de la Cruz, both of Tenerife's airports, Santa Cruz, La Candelaria, the Mount Teide cable car bottom station, Gran Canaria airport and La Palma airport.
Calle de San Francisco. Tel: (922) 382855.
Closed: Sat afternoon.

You'll find souvenirs to suit all tastes

Entertainment

You're never short on quantity of entertainment in large holiday resorts, but the quality may be disappointing. It is often a choice between uninspired international cabaret shows, and grotesque home-from-home 'fun pubs'. Fortunately there is another parallel cultural world on both Gran Canaria and Tenerife, one which exploits the best home grown creativity but also welcomes international performers of standing. You may, however, have to travel into the capital city of the island you are on to take advantage of it.

A night on the town

'Highbrow' cultural events are not advertised to tourists, but the tourist information offices will tell you what's on. Spectator sports can also be worth seeking out (*see p152*), particularly traditional competitions of pole jumping, stick wrestling, plough lifting and stone throwing.

The English-language newspaper, *Tenerife News*, is a good source of information about forthcoming events and in it you can also find out about original version films that are shown. If you want more informal entertainment that is locally authentic, ask around. Chances are that the musicians trotting out the timeless classics for tourists in the hotel lounge will themselves retreat to some small bar where a decent live band is playing.

Casinos

Gran Canaria has two casinos and Tenerife three. French and American roulette, blackjack, and craps are the most common games. The rules are explained in detail every night before each session (from around 8pm–5am), though neither the fear of losing nor the late hours should stop you from playing. Two common-sense rules to cut your losses are to decide on your limit in advance and stick to it rigidly, and leave your credit cards at the hotel.

You will need your passport, and you must be dressed smartly (though not necessarily in jacket and tie) to be allowed admission.

The grandest and oldest place to play is the **Casino Taoro**, perched high in its own landscaped grounds above Puerto de la Cruz on Tenerife (*Tel: (922) 380550*). It's the sort of place where you might expect to meet James Bond during one of his thrilling escapades.

Other casinos on Tenerife are the **Casino Santa Cruz** in the Hotel Mencey, Santa Cruz (*Tel: (922) 276700*), and the **Casino Playa de las Américas** in the Gran Tinerfe Hotel (*Tel: (922) 793758*).

The most impressively sited casino on Gran Canaria is that of **Las Palmas**

Casino in the Santa Catalina Hotel in Doramas Parque (*Tel: (928) 243040*). The island's other gaming palace is **Casino Gran Canaria** in the Hotel Meliá Tamarindos in San Agustín (*Tel: (928) 774090*).

Nightlife
Nightspots in the Canary Islands come in two kinds: those that offer a full meal and live variety entertainment and those that aim to attract a young crowd with deafening (recorded) music. The epicentres of the latter, that is of the islands' pulsating 18–30 nightlife are **Playa de las Américas** (Tenerife) and **Playa del Inglés** (Gran Canaria). The Verónicas area of Playa de las Américas is notorious for attracting trouble.

Elsewhere, Puerto de la Cruz in Tenerife and Puerto Rico in Gran Canaria provide the best choice of *discotecas* on the islands. If there is an admission charge, then it will normally cover the first drink. Most stay open until 3am, but some discotecas go on much later.

Shows
The only common denominator between most shows (*espectáculos*) put on in holiday areas of the islands is a no-frills, robust attitude to tourist family entertainment. The largest hotels usually have a busy programme of live music and variety performances for guests only but some are open to non-residents.

Nightspots stay open until the wee hours in Playa de las Américas

GRAN CANARIA
Sioux City (*see p55*), a transplanted chunk of the wild west which stages barbecues and a saloon show.

Casino Palace Dinner Show
Probably the most famous show on Gran Canaria.
Hotel Meliá Tamarindos, San Agustín.

TENERIFE
Andrómeda
Nightclub in Lago Martiánez (*see p88*).
Puerto de la Cruz. Tel: (922) 383852.

Castillo San Miguel
A night of medieval-style jousting.
San Miguel Aldea Blanca, 15km east of Playa de las Américas.
Tel: (928) 700276.

Fiesta Canaria Carnaval
The next best thing to the real Carnaval (*see pp20–21*).
Calle Las Toscas, 99, Santa Catalina, Tacoronte. Tel: (922) 382910.

Fiestas and Festivals
Traditional fiestas (*see pp18–19*) offer plenty of entertainment including live music, dancing and street parades for free. The Canary Islands Music Festival takes place in January and February. From April to June Las Palmas holds the Alfredo Kraus Opera Festival and in November the free Womad (World of Music, Arts and Dance) festival. Jazz festivals are held in Puerto de Mogán, Gran Canaria, in March, and in La Laguna, Tenerife (Oct/Nov). Maspalomas puts on a film festival in November.

Flamenco
Though thought of as 'typically Spanish', flamenco song and dance is native to far away Andalucia and has nothing to do with the Canaries. Flamenco, however, does travel and shows are regularly staged by the top hotels. Wherever you see it, a good flamenco troupe is

Busker on Calle Mayor de Triana, Las Palmas

always a treat. Look for signs in bars and restaurants. Flamenco shows are staged at **Parque de Las Américas** at Playa de las Américas, near Hotel Gran Tinerfe in Tenerife *Tel: (922) 797611*.

Folklore

Canarian folklore shows are gentle but enjoyable family affairs, with large groups of musicians accompanying a dance troupe in traditional costume. The rhythms are generally Spanish, and played on guitars, flutes, and the *timple*, a small ukulele-like instrument.

The best shows are staged in the **Pueblo Canario** in Las Palmas de Gran Canaria (*see pp28 and 30*). Worth catching on Tenerife is the Sunday morning show at the **Hotel Tigaiga**, Puerto de la Cruz, Tenerife (*Tel: (922) 383500*), which includes a demonstration of *lucha canaria* (Canarian wrestling).

Performing Arts

The best venues are in the capitals of Tenerife and Gran Canaria, although culture does stray to other parts of the islands. Santa Cruz's most prestigious concert hall is the **Auditorio de Tenerife** (*see p66*). The city's other main venue is the **Teatro Guimerá**, Plaza Isla de la Madera (*Tel: (902) 364603*).

In Las Palmas, the **Auditorio Alfredo Kraus** (*see p28*) provides an impressive setting for concerts and opera, as does the **Teatro Pérez Galdós** (*Tel: (928) 361509*).

The Gran Canaria Philharmonic Orchestra and the Tenerife Symphony Orchestra play concerts year round.

Street entertainment in Puerto de la Cruz

Children

The Spanish love children and both Gran Canaria and Tenerife are geared up for family tourism. The smaller islands, in contrast, have little to offer kids, although they may enjoy the boat journey over to La Gomera and back. A simple change from the beach and sea may be to hire a bike and pedal around your resort; a more unusual way to get around the neighbouring countryside is on a camel's back. If you want a full family day out there are theme parks and animals parks galore in southern and northern Tenerife, and in southern Gran Canaria.

Funfair at *Carnaval*

It can be hard to combine an adult interest in sightseeing with something for the kids to do, but one way may be to take the cable car to the top of Mount Teide (*see pp96–9*).

If you just want an informal holiday with the kids, you'll find that child-friendly hotels and restaurants are the norm and some even lay on suitable night-time entertainment for children. You can also use Spain's penchant for festivities to your advantage: ask about local fiestas and you'll almost certainly stumble upon some spectacle worth watching. Most are in the summer months, but during *Carnaval* season in January and February (*see pp20–1*) there is usually a gaudy parade going on with loud live music.

'Safaris'

There are plenty of stables offering riding lessons for children, but a more novel way to go is on the back of a camel. There are two camel safari centres near Fataga on Gran Canaria

(*see p50*) and one at El Tanque on Tenerife. Whale and dolphin 'safaris' on Tenerife, meanwhile, may well appeal to older children. (*see pp134–5*).

Waterparks

The four waterparks on Gran Canaria and Tenerife may not be in the Florida-style big league but they will probably provide almost as much amusement. Maspalomas has two: **Aqualand** (*see p54*) and the much smaller **Ocean Park**. On Tenerife there is an Aqualand near Playa de las Américas on the Cosa Adeje (*see pp102–3*).

Watersports

If your water babies are old enough to windsurf, you may well be able to find tuition and small boards at one of the many schools on the islands (*see Sport pp150–3*). Otherwise 'water bananas' and 'ringos' (inflatables pulled behind a speedboat) splash along at Puerto Rico (Gran Canaria), and Playa de las

Américas (Tenerife). Pedaloes are also available here.

Wildlife

The two larger islands have several well-run bird and wildlife parks. By far the biggest and best is the Florida-style **Loro Parque** at Puerto de la Cruz on Tenerife (*see pp88–9*), but close behind is **Palmitos Parque,** an excellent bird and butterfly park on Gran Canaria (*see p54*). Other places to visit are **Reptilandia** at Galdar (*see p39*), which specialises in creepy-crawlies, the crocodile-infested **Cocodrilo Park** (*see p44*) and perhaps **Cactualdea** (*see*

p58) which puts on family-orientated shows explaining Canary Island traditions.

Theme Parks

Loro Parque and **Palmitos Park** are theme parks of a sort and **Holiday World** at Maspalomas has conventional rides to go on. **Sioux City** (*see p55*), outside Maspalomas, is a rowdy Wild West spectacle. Las Palmas' **Pueblo Canario** (*see pp28–30*), and Puerto de la Cruz's **Pueblo Chico** (*see pp82–3*) and **Mundo Aborigen** (*p55*) all aim to teach children about Canary Island traditions.

Kids love the *Carnaval* in Santa Cruz de Tenerife

Sport and Leisure

The Canaries' climate favours an outdoor life and the islands are ever popular with both professional and amateur sports enthusiasts. There is plenty of choice if you want to get outside and do something physical, even if only to break the routine of lying on the beach. Watersports inevitably predominate, but land-based sports are increasing in popularity. Golfers in particular will find both quantity and quality on Gran Canaria and even more so on Tenerife. There are few sporting facilities (on or off the water) on the smaller islands. For biking and walking *see pp137–8.*

Go cycling on La Gomera

Windsurfing and Waterskiing

The windy conditions are a plus factor for experienced boardsailers, and Tenerife is one of the world's favourite windsurfing destinations. But there are plenty of sheltered bays where, with a little tuition, beginners can stand upright on a board or on waterskis. The principal watersports centre is Puerto Rico on Gran Canaria, but the south of Tenerife also has much to offer.

Deep Sea Fishing

Shark, barracuda, swordfish, sailfish, marlin, tuna and even stingray are all on the big-game menu for the fishermen who charter craft from the many marinas on the islands. The most productive fishing grounds are off the south coast of Gran Canaria, where over 30 world records have been claimed for various types of fish. If you want to check out the most successful boats, find out what time they return to the marina and see the fishermen pose alongside their catch of the day for the photo-album picture.

The principal charter marinas are: Las Palmas (Santa Catalina pier), Pasito Blanco, Puerto Rico and Playa Blanca on Gran Canaria; and Los Cristianos and Puerto Colón (Playa de la Américas) on Tenerife.

Diving

Diving is very popular in the Canary Islands because of their warm, clear waters. Marine life, wrecks, and reefs are not as prolific here as in other more exotic diving destinations in the world, but underwater parks have been designated at Arinaga, off the east coast of Gran Canaria. All the clubs below give tuition.

GRAN CANARIA
La Tortuga
Enables disabled people to go diving.
Calle Cordoba, 57-4B, Las Palmas.
Tel: (928) 336126.

Náutico
Classes for all abilities.
Daily dives. Training in
swimming pool and sea.
*Hotel IFA-Interclub
Atlantic, San Agustin.
Tel: (928) 778168.*

Sun Sub
Courses in various
languages. Daily dives
from coast or boat.
*Hotel Buenaventura Playa.
Tel: (928) 778165.*

Top Diving
Operates two boats of 8m
and 6m respectively.
*Puerto Rico. Tel: (928)
560609.*

TENERIFE
Barrakuda
Open all year. Dives up to
30m. Night dives possible.
*Hotel Paraíso Floral, Playa
Paraiso Adeje.
Tel: (922) 741881.*

Gruber
Fifteen dive sites up to
40m serviced by a hard
boat.
*Hotel Park Club Europe,
Playa de las Américas.
Tel: (922) 752708.*

Ecosub
Dives to the underwater
caves and volcanic tubes
and arches of the north
coast.

*Calle Cologán, 14, Puerto
de la Cruz. Tel: (922)
371731.*

Sailing
Boats of various sizes can
be hired from several
sports marinas (*puerto
deportivo*) around the
islands.
   Below are some of the
principal marinas, local
sailing clubs, and
federations.

GRAN CANARIA
**Las Palmas de Gran
Canaria Marina**
Tel: (928) 300480.

**Pasito Blanco Yachting
Club**
*Carretera C–812 km 60,
San Bartolomé de
Tirajana.
Tel: (928) 142194.*

Anfi del Mar Marina
*Barranco de la Verga,
Mogán.
Tel: (928) 150798.*

Puerto Rico Marina
Tel: (928) 561141.

TENERIFE
Marina San Miguel
*Urbanización Amarilla
Golf, San Miguel de
Abona.
Tel: (922) 785124.*

ECC Yacht Charter
*Miraflores, 19, Santa Cruz
de Tenerife.
Tel: (922) 240559.*

**WSC Water Sports &
Charters Nautiocio
Tenerife**
*Escuela Naútica de Puerto
Colón, Costa Adeje.
Tel: (922) 715457.*

Surfing
Both Gran Canaria and
Tenerife have numerous
spots for surfing and
bodyboarding. Wherever
you go, don't forget the
golden rule: never surf
alone.

Golf
Tenerife has nine golf
courses to choose from
and Gran Canaria six, of
which the main ones are
listed here. The quality is
generally good. Most
clubs have a driving
range, practice putting
green, club and trolley
hire, and clubhouse.

GRAN CANARIA
**Campo de Golf
Maspalomas**
Beautiful location on the
edge of the dunes and the
oasis. 18 holes, 6,216m.
*Avenida TO Neckermann.
Tel: (928) 762581.*

Cortijo
An 18-hole course is 6km from Las Palmas, and 10 minutes from the airport. *Autopista GS 1km 6, 4, Telde.* *Tel: (928) 711111.*

Real Club de Golf de Las Palmas (Club Bandama)
This century-old club was the first ever to be formed on Spanish territory, and enjoys a magnificent setting on the edge of the Caldera de Bandama. 18 holes, 5,679m. *Santa Brígida, 14km southwest of Las Palmas.* *Tel: (928) 353354.*

Salobre Golf
18-hole course nestled in the hills behind Pasito Blanco near Maspalomas. *Autopista GC 1km 53.* *Tel: (928) 010103.*

TENERIFE
Real Club de Tenerife
18 holes. *Tel: (922) 636607.*

Golf Club Amarilla
18 holes. *Amarilla Country Club, San Miguel de Abona.* *Tel: (922) 730319.* *www.amarillagolf.es*

Golf del Sur
Home to the Tenerife

Open. Handicap necessary. 27 holes. *San Miguel de Abona, Tel: (922) 738170.*

El Peñón
18 holes. *Tacoronte.* *Tel: (922) 636607.* *Reservation essential for non-members.*

Las Americas
18 holes. *Tel: (922) 752005.*

Costa Adeje
27 holes. *Tel: (922) 710000.*

Tecina Golf
18 holes. *Tel: (922) 145950.*

Buenavista
18 holes. *Tel: (922) 129034.*

Tennis
Many larger hotels have tennis courts that are hired out to the public. Tennis centres in Tenerife include: **Hotel Las Palmeras**, Playa de las Américas, where tuition and floodlit courts are available *Tel: (922) 752948.* **Tenisur**, San Eugenio *Tel: (922) 796167.* In Gran Canaria the **Tennis Centre**

Maspalomas also has gym facilities. *Tel: (928) 767447.*

Spectator Sports
Football
Tenerife Football has hosted the likes of Barcelona and Real Madrid at its home ground in Santa Cruz. Matches are usually on a Saturday evening or a Sunday. See the local papers for details.

Sailing (*Vela Latina*)
On Gran Canaria, traditional Canarian sailing lateens (small crafts with large triangular sails) race off Las Palmas and Puerto Rico on Saturday afternoons and Sunday mornings between April and September.

Wrestling (*Lucha Canaria*)
This traditional fighting sport is likely to appeal to fans of Sumo wrestling. The basic objective is to throw your opponent to the ground, but there are other rituals to be observed. The sport is active on all the islands and most villages have a team comprising 12 wrestlers.

The pool at the Parador Nacional, San Sebastián

Café Life

If you want to see real Canarians at play, just walk into any busy café, buy a coffee or a beer and take a ringside seat. Cafés are usually fairly spartan, noisy, recreational meeting areas, male-oriented (although women do go there, too), and tolerant of children any time of the day or night.

Spain is known to be one of the noisiest places in the world, and many Canarian cafés seem to take it upon themselves to uphold this tradition. The television can be on from the day's first children's cartoon, through the dreadful afternoon soap operas, to the evening game shows. Hardly anyone is watching, and most probably cannot hear what is going on anyway, owing to the radio behind the bar, or the fruit machine in the corner filling the whole café with loud electronic tones. No wonder the locals shout and gesticulate at each other – it's the only way to be heard!

The only time the TV really draws the audience is when a football match is on. CD Tenerife are the local favourites; otherwise the crowd will cheer for Barcelona, or indeed anyone else who will put Real Madrid's nose out of joint.

Locals may add to the cacophony by striking the metal bar with coins to grab the attention of the barmen. Alcoholic drinks are served at any time, in devil-may-care measures, though most locals start the day with a *café solo* (black coffee). Tourists generally order *café con leche* (coffee with milk), while those who want an alternative between harsh black and sweet or milky white, opt for a *cortado* (small with a little milk). Donuts (it's the same word) and *tostada* (toast) are usually available for breakfast.

After a quick scan of the papers and a word to their friends, those who have work to go to, depart. Those who don't, and the older retired men, sit down for a game of dominoes or cards; and around midday the *tapas* (a quarter of a portion of a normal meal) is unveiled and eaten.

Whichever island you choose, there will always be somewhere to sit and watch the world go by

Food and Drink

Canarian food is tasty, fresh and filling, though rarely glamorous. Unfortunately, on the larger islands, it is usually easier to find a 'Real British Pub' or a fast-food restaurant than a Canarian *típico* (typical native restaurant). The latter is distinguished by a relatively short menu of soups, stews, and grilled fish dishes. If you can't find a *típico*, the best alternative for local food is a place serving tapas. This is the Spanish custom of serving small portions of local food in informal restaurant or bar surroundings. Tapas bars, however, are also quite thin on the ground in the tourist centres.

Local sausages from Teror

Canarian Cuisine

Canarian cuisine is essentially peasant and fishermen's food. Meat usually features as part of a stew (normally pork, veal, or rabbit). Steaks, generally imported from Spain or South America, are for tourists only.

Soupy stews are the most typical Canarian meals. *Potaje* has only vegetables; add meat to make *rancho*

Canarian cheese for sale in Cruz de Tejeda

canario, and add more meat still to make *puchero*. This is, of course, a generalisation; each is flavoured differently, with herbs such as thyme, saffron, marjoram, parsley, and particularly cumin and coriander, but basic ingredients are similar. A Guanche staple, *gofio* (maize meal), once eaten as bread, is still used to thicken stews. Another common stew is *garbanzo compuesto* (chick-pea stew with meat), often available as a tapas.

Other typical Canarian casserole dishes are sancocho, a stew of salted fish (often seabass), and *conejo con salmorejo* (rabbit in a spicy, tomato-based sauce).

Fresh fish is always on the menu, and seaside restaurants can offer a bewildering and untranslatable fish list (although it's rarely the case that everything listed on the menu is available). The method of cooking is usually plain – either boiled, fried, or grilled (often on a barbecue). As an accompaniment you will be served salad and *papas arrugadas* ('wrinkled potatoes'). The latter are small potatoes, boiled in their jackets in very salty water. On the table there will be two cold olive oil-based sauces; red *mojo picón* (piquant sauce) and *mojo verde* (green sauce). The latter is a cool parsley and coriander sauce, perfect with fish; the former is a spicy chilli and paprika mix, generally poured over potatoes and/or red meat.

The most famous Canarian dessert is *bienmesabe*, a concoction of honey, almonds, and rum. Despite its frequent appearance on menus, it is rarely available, and you may have to make do with the ubiquitous Spanish *flan* (a cooked milk dessert, like crème caramel).

Do try the local cheese, wherever you are. This is always made from goats' milk, and is invariably good.

Drinks

Both Gran Canaria and Tenerife make reasonable red and white wines. La Palma is famous for its Malvasia-style wines, grown on the volcanic soil. These come in dry as well as sweet styles and are good quality, the best being rich and full-bodied. Canarian after-dinner drinks include *mistela* (a sweet wine),

Sancocho
This is a popular dish with the Canarians, made up of herbs, salted fish, sweet potatoes, and vegetables, all cooked together.
Papas Arrugadas (wrinkled potatoes). Small potatoes in their skins are boiled with rock salt (a lot) and then served with hot paprika, with chilli sauce poured over them.

Try a drop of the *ron miel* (rum honey)

and *parra* (a firewater-style aguardiente brandy), though these are not common. *Ron miel* (rum-honey) is to be found everywhere. White cane-spirit rum is made on Gran Canaria; the 'honey' is actually sap from the palm tree, gathered in La Gomera. The resultant cocktail is a pleasant, smooth, orange-tasting drink, resembling neither conventional rum nor honey!

Where to Eat
Eating out is relatively inexpensive. In the resorts, competition tends to keep prices down, and in the villages, eating out

Plenty to choose from on this menu

is generally priced for the locals. If you don't mind fairly basic amenities and a menu with little choice, and you can manage a little Spanish, the latter is nearly always better value and more enjoyable. Portions are usually large, and a typical Canarian soup-stew starter may well suffice as a main course.

In the listings of recommended restaurants the approximate cost of a three-course meal per person with a half-bottle of wine, or a couple of beers, is indicated by the following symbols:

*	up to €15
**	€15–20
***	€20–30
****	over €30

GRAN CANARIA
Las Palmas de Gran Canaria
Ca'Cho Damian★★
Canarian cuisine including tasty soups. Long bar serving a variety of tapas.
Centro Comercial La Ballena, 26–28.
Tel: (928) 417300.
El Cerdo Que Ríe★★
Friendly restaurant, famous for its Spanish food, fondues, and flambés. It also serves

international cuisine.
Paseo de Las Canteras, 31–35.
Tel: (928) 244954.
La Parilla★★★★
Superb international cuisine in this 5-star hotel.
Hotel Reina Isabel, Calle Alfredo L Jones, 40.
Tel: (928) 260100.
La Marinera★★★
The fish is excellent in this restaurant which uses only fresh ingredients to prepare a varied selection of dishes.
Alonso Ojeda.
Tel: (928) 464265.
Amaiur★★★★
Authentic Basque cuisine in one of the best restaurants in Las Palmas.
Pérez Galdós, 2.
Tel: (928) 370717.
Mesón la Cuadra H★
This restaurant offers a great variety of tapas, or a simple but tasty menu cooked with ingredients grown by the owner.
General Mas de Gaminde, 32.
Tel: (928) 243380.
El Cucharón★★★★
Sophisticated restaurant specialising in creative cuisine and sophisticated dishes.
Reloj, 2.
Tel: (928) 333296.

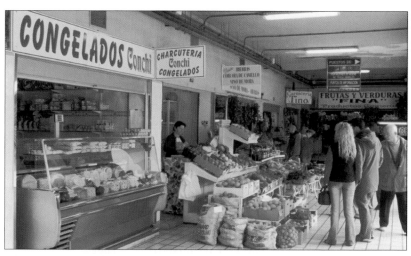

Pick up some provisions from the covered market in Santa Cruz

Agaete
Casa Pepe★★
As well as serving the typical *mojos* and *papas arrugadas*, this restaurant also offers excellent fish.
Alcalde Armas Galván, 5.
Tel: (928) 898227.
Dedo de Dios★★
Bright, airy fish restaurant with views of the impressive Dedo de Dios rock stack.
Ctra. Puerto de las Nieves (Puerto de las Nieves).
Tel: (928) 898581.

Agüimes
La Farola★★/★★★
Excellent fresh fish.
Alcalá Galiano, 3 (Playa de Arinaga).
Tel: (928) 180410.

Arucas
El Mesón de la Montaña★★★
This restaurant with great views serves a great variety of high quality Canarian dishes.
Montaña de Arucas.
Tel: (928) 600844.

Cruz de Tejeda
Restaurante Asador Grill Yolanda★★
Excellent and inventive Canarian specialities served in this typical Canarian restaurant.
Cruz de Tejeda.
Tel: (928) 666276.

Puerto de Mogán
Restaurante Tu Casa★★
A very popular restaurant serving Canary cuisine prepared with fresh ingredients.
Avenida Artes, 18.
Tel: (928) 565078.

Maspalomas
El Portalón★★★★
This excellent restaurant specialises in high quality Basque cuisine.
Av. Tirajana, 27, Playa del Inglés-San Agustín.
Tel: (928) 771622.
La Toja★★★
Small, pleasant restaurant, superb Galician dishes.
Edificio Barbados, Av. Tirajana, 17, Playa del Inglés-San Agustín.
Tel: (928) 761196.

TENERIFE
Santa Cruz de Tenerife
Amós★★★★
Exquisite Canary cuisine
and a fair variety of
international dishes. Try
the shrimp salad with
black potatoes.
Poeta Tomás Morales, 2.
Tel: (922) 285001.
La Cazuela★★★★
Mediterranean traditions
inspire the creativity of
the chef, producing dishes
like cold lasagne with
goat's cheese, avocados
and peppers. For desert:
watermelon jelly.
Robayna, 34.
Tel: (922) 272300.
Viva Mexico★★★
The perfect place to
savour enchiladas and
burritos, amongst a wide
selection of other
Mexican dishes.
Santa Clara, 8.
Tel: (922) 296088.
El Líbano★★★
For twenty years this
restaurant has been
serving excellent
Lebanese cuisine and
traditional Arabian
dishes. Takeaway service.
Santiago Cuadrado, 36.
Tel: (922) 285914.
La Posada★★
Asturian and Canary
cooking are the preserve
of this restaurant, which

also offers a huge variety
of tapas and good
selection of wines. Closed
Mon.
Méndez Núñez, 61.
Tel: (922) 246772.

Los Cristianos
El Sol★★★
Classic French cuisine is
prepared by the owner-
chef of this popular
restaurant.
Playa de los Cristianos.
Tel: (922) 790569.

Barranco del Infierno
(Adeje)
Otelo★★
This restaurant stands at
the entrance to the
Barranco del Infierno, of
which there is a
magnificent view from
the terrace. Specialities
include chicken and
rabbit. Closed Tue.
Los Molinos, 44.
Tel: (922) 780374.

Cañadas del Teide
Parador de Las Cañadas
del Teide★★★
The dining room of the
parador in the national
park (*see pp96–9*) serves
superb Canarian dishes in
a magnificent setting.
Parador de Las Cañadas
del Teide.
Tel: (922) 374841.

El Sauzal
Casa del Vino la
Baranda★★/★★★
This restaurant belongs
to a wine museum
(*see p83*). It offers a
good selection of
contemporary Canary
dishes based on
traditional ingredients.
Autopista del Norte, km
21.
Tel: (922) 56388.

Garachico
Isla Baja★★
A popular fish restaurant,
overlooking the seafront.
Calle Esteban de Ponte, 5.
Tel: (922) 830008.

Puerto de la Cruz
Casa de Miranda★★★★
Elegant first-floor
restaurant in historic
18th-century house.
Lighter dishes and tapas
served in the ground-
floor bodega.
Calle Santo Domingo, 13,
Plaza de Europa.
Tel: (922) 373871.
Mario★★/★★★
Small fish restaurant in
the pretty Rincón del
Puerto courtyard
complex. Closed Mon.
Edificio Rincón del Puerto,
Plaza El Charco.
Tel: (922) 385535.

LA GOMERA
San Sebastián de la Gomera
Parador de La Gomera★★★★
Superb innovative Canarian dishes in this island parador.
Balcón de la Villa y Puerto.
Tel: (922) 871100.
Casa del Mar★
An unpretentious and inexpensive restaurant serving mainly simple seafood dishes.
Avenida Fred Olsen, 2.
Tel: (922) 870320.

Valle Gran Rey
Restaurante-Escuela Mirador César Manrique★★★
Gomeran recipes made with locally-produced products. Try the rabbit chops with Port wine.
Carretera General.
Tel: (922) 805868.

LA PALMA
Santa Cruz de la Palma
Chipi Chipi★★
Attractive garden restaurant famous for its barbecued fish and meats.
Juan Mayor, 42.
Tel: (922) 411024.
Canarias★
Functional but friendly modern seafront establishment offering good-value Canarian dishes.
Avenida Marítima 28.
Tel: (922) 411000.

Breña Baja
Parador de la Palma★★
The parador's restaurant is always a good bet to try traditional Canary cuisine.
Carretera del Zumacal.
Tel: (922) 435828.

El Paso
Bodegón Tamanca★
Rustic cave bar serving local food in generous helpings.
Las Manchas (10km south of Los Llanos de Ariadne)
Tel: (922) 494002.

EL HIERRO
Valverde
El Mirador de la Peña★★
Canarian and island specialities are served in tranquil surroundings with panoramic views.
Carretera General Guarazoca, 40.
Tel: (922) 550300.
Parador del Hierro★★
The restaurant in this modern parador serves traditional local food and regional cuisine from other parts of Spain.
Las Playas, 15.
Tel: (922) 558036.
La Higuera de la Abuela★★
Simple Canary Island food washed down with a fine selection of local wines.
Tajinis Coba, 3.
Tel: (922) 551026.

Nature's fast food

Hotels and Accommodation

The vast majority of tourist accommodation on Gran Canaria and Tenerife – especially in the south of the two islands – has been built over the last 30 years to cater for package holidaymakers. But increasingly the trend has between towards small hotels of character which offer peace and quiet and a personal service, making for much greater choice for the independent traveller looking for more than a beach hotel with a swimming pool.

Exotic places to stay

Hotels

Spanish hotels are ranked from one to five stars although these classifications are awarded according to a checklist of amenities not according to their inherent charm or the friendliness of their staff.

Pick up any holiday brochure and you will find page upon page of characterless Canarian hotels, all built to a similar three- or four-star standard. These provide comfortable, well-equipped rooms, a swimming pool, bars, possibly a discotheque, live nightly entertainments, sports facilities, boutiques and so on. Many of these are large (around 300 rooms), and high-rise, and a good number are still raw around the edges.

Cheap hotels (below a three-star grading) are thin on the ground. Try Las Palmas, Santa Cruz de Tenerife and Puerto de la Cruz.

Travellers putting together their own package in three- or four-star hotels (or apartments) are advised to book well ahead and shop around for prices.

The hotels' stated nightly rates often bear little resemblance to what may be negotiated. In general, however, it would be difficult to beat the price of a late availability package.

Note that many hotels quote rates without tax which is roughly 10 per cent of the price.

Residencia means a hotel that does not serve meals on the premises – although it may do breakfasts.

Hostales and Pensións

Hostales – designated by the sign Hs – are of a lower standard than hotels, and are graded from one to three stars. Facilities in a three-star *hostal* should be the equivalent of a reasonable two-star hotel, but don't expect much in one- or two-star places.

In theory, a *pensión* (guesthouse), is even humbler than a *hostal* but official classifications can easily mislead. Both *hostales* and *pensións* are relatively rare in the Canary Islands. The best places to look are in the older cities and towns rather than tourist resorts, especially Las

Palmas de Gran Canaria, Santa Cruz de Tenerife and Puerto de la Cruz.

Hotelapartamentos

Hotelapartamentos, or aparthotels, feature rooms with their own kitchen facilities, yet retain most of the other trappings of an ordinary hotel. These are popular in most large resorts, and a good bet for families with children.

Time Share

Time share is a much maligned accommodation option, largely on account of the unsavoury get-rich-quick characters it seems to attract. Most time-share organisations offer exchange facilities, should you tire of your original choice, or need to change.

There are no specific rules that apply to buying time-share packages in the Canaries that don't apply generally anywhere else. The two golden rules to apply are: never sign anything while on holiday (get home and 'cool off' first), or without sound legal advice. It would

also seem common sense to avoid the overtures of the often loutish street-corner touts.

Paradors

Paradors are state-run hotels distributed throughout the whole of Spain which aim to reflect the regions which they serve in both their architecture and their cuisine. Wherever possible they occupy existing buildings of historical importance; otherwise they are purpose-built but set in stunning natural locations. *Paradors* often, but not always, provide the best accommodation and service in a region but even when they are outmatched they still offer consistency and reliability. *Paradors'* room rates vary, and while they are generally up-market there are often special deals to be had.

The best (and most expensive) *parador* in the Canaries is the mock-colonial Parador de la Gomera, an attraction in its own right, and recognised as one of the finest small

A room with a view on La Gomera

paradores in all Spain. Tenerife's Cañadas del Teide *parador* resembles a mountain chalet, cosy and popular with walkers. The *parador* in Santa Cruz de La Palma, meanwhile, merges seamlessly with the town's traditional seafront houses. If you really want to get away from the crowds, El Hierro's modern-traditional *parador*, set at the end of a road going nowhere on the loneliest island of them all, is the last word in solitude. All, apart from Santa Cruz, have their own swimming pools.

For central bookings contact Paradores de Turismo de España, Requena 3, 28013 Madrid. Tel: (91) 515 6666.
www.parador.es
In the UK contact Keytel International, 402 Edgware Road, London W2 1ED. Tel: (020) 7616 0300. www.keytel.co.uk enquiries@keytel.co.uk.
In other countries, enquire at the Spanish National Tourist Office (see pp185–6).

Rural Hotels
Small hotels, lovingly restored and run, are springing up in the more rural parts of Gran Canaria and Tenerife. *For information contact the Asociación Canaria de Turismo Rural (www.ecoturismocanarias.com) or see the website: www.toprural.com*

Self-Catering
Self-catering bungalows and apartments are a popular holiday choice in the Canary Islands, and are usually grouped together in developments known as *urbanizaciones*. These also often include time-share apartments.

If you would like an apartment away from the tourist ghettos, ask the local tourist office for details (many of these are only for rent for a minimum period of a month), or, before you go, consult one of the smaller specialist island operators.

Youth Hostels
There are no youth hostels or similar associations on the islands. La Palma has a hostal at San Antonio de Monte which is available for groups only. *Tel: (922) 400444.*

Camping
Given the ideal climate for camping, sites are surprisingly few and far between. There are only three official sites on the islands, but *camping sauvage* (wild camping – off-site) is tolerated in many places. Enquire at the local tourist office to reduce the chance of being moved on by jealous farmers or possessive landowners.

Tenerife has just one official site: the well-equipped Nauta at Las Galletas, Arona, on the south coast (*Tel: (922) 785118*). The island also has two municipal campsites at Punta del Hidalgo in the Montes de Anaga (*Tel: (629) 139203*) and at Playa de la Arena in Tacoronte (*Tel: (669) 811534*). If you do see backpackers on southern Tenerife it is likely they are off to La Gomera – probably to the Valle Gran Rey, popular with campers and those in search of an alternative lifestyle.

There is one designated site on La Gomera, at Caserio de Cedro on the edge of the Garajonay National Park. This is administered by the island government office, and if you wish to camp here you should contact the office in San Sebastián de La Gomera, Carretera General del Sur, 20. *Tel: (922) 870105.*

Camping within the national park on La Gomera is strictly forbidden, as it is in the Teide National Park on Tenerife, although here climbers and keen walkers may apply to use the spartan mountain refuge at Altavista (ask for information at one of the park's information centres).

La Palma has six designated campsites. One of these is in the national park below Roque Salvaje, an hour and a half's walk from Los Brecitos. Maximum stay is two nights and permission must be sought in advance by telephoning *(922) 497277*. The other sites are at Fuencaliente (one night only, *Tel: (922) 411593*), El Pilar (*Tel: (922) 411583*), La Laguna de Barlovento (*Tel: (922) 696023*), La Rosa (*Tel: (922) 493306*) and Santo Domingo de Garafia (one night only, *Tel: (922) 411593*).

Gran Canaria has two official sites: Guantánamo at Playa Tauro near Mogán (*Tel: (928) 560207*), and Temisas, Lomo de la Cruz, on the road from Agüimes to San Bartolomé de Tirajana (*Tel: (928) 798149*). Both are well equipped. Unofficial sites include one at Pasito Blanco and another at Fataga (ask at local tourist offices for details).

There are no official sites on El Hierro.

For further information about camping in the Canary Islands contact the **Federación Española de Empresarios de Campings**, *San Bernardo 97-99, Edificio Colomina 3°, 28015 Madrid. Tel: (91) 448 1234. fedcamping@hotmail.com www.fedcamping.com*

The packed hill-side in San Sebastián

Reservations

It is advisable to book in advance. You can book through your travel agent or by calling or emailing the hotel directly. Be prepared to give a credit card number over the phone to reserve a room. On arrival you will be expected to show your passport. You should vacate your room at noon on the day of your departure or you may be charged for an extra night.

Prices

The guide prices here are based on a typical double room, including tax but not normally breakfast.

*	under €50
**	€50–100
***	€100–150
****	€150–250
*****	over €250

GRAN CANARIA

Casa de Los Camellos★★

A charming hotel in Agüimes in a building once used as a granary to feed merchants' camels. Its 12 double rooms furnished with antiques are grouped around a double inner patio.
Progreso, 12, 35260 Agüimes. Tel: (928) 785003.
www.hecansa.com

Cortijo de San Ignacio Golf ★★

An 18th-century country house with its own 18-hole golf course. It has 16 double rooms and 2 single rooms.
Autopista del Sur GC1 km. 6,400, 35218 Telde. Tel: (928) 712427.
www.cortijosanignaciogolf.com

El Refugio★★

Rural hotel on the Cruz de Tejeda crossroads which can be busy with trippers during the day but is peaceful at night. Ten comfortable bedrooms. Private parking, swimming pool, mini-golf, mountain bikes and horses for hire.
Cruz de Tejeda s/n, 35328 Tejeda. Tel: (928) 666513.
www.hotelruralelrefugio.com

Finca Las Longueras★★

Also known by the locals as the 'Red House', this large colonial manor is situated in the centre of a plantation of oranges, avocados and papayas in the Valle de Agaete.
Valle de Agaete, 35480 Agaete. Tel. (928) 898145.
www.laslongueras.com

Gloria Palace San Agustín★★★★

Luxury complex for thalassotherapy (spa treatment with sea water), with its own Turkish bath, spa and massage rooms.
Las Margaritas, s/n, Playa de San Agustín, 35100 Maspalomas. Tel: (928) 128500. www.hotelgloriapalace.com

Gran Hotel Costa Meloneras★★★★

Luxury spa hotel on Maspalomas beach built to an oriental theme and including unusual features such as ice walls and a salt-water lagoon.
Mar Mediterráneo, 1, 35100 Maspalomas. Tel: (928) 128100.
www.ghcmeloneras.com

La Hacienda del Buen Suceso★★★

The Marquis of Arucas' 18th-century farmhouse stands in the middle of a banana plantation upon which absolute silence descends at night. Dining room and heated swimming pool.
Finca del Buen Suceso, Carretera de Arucas a Bañaderos, km 1, 53400 Arucas. Tel: (928) 622945.
www.haciendabuensuceso.com

Las Calas★★

A small, homely farmhouse down a windy lane off the Las Palmas–Cruz de Tejeda road through the island. Informal but very comfortable.

El Arenal, 36, La Lechuza, 35320 Vega de San Mateo. Tel: (928) 661436.
www.hotelrurallascalas.com

Las Tirajanas★★/★★★

This spa hotel on a hill above the town of San Bartolomé de Tirajana has tremendous views from its rooms over the mountains, down the Barranco Fataga and as far as Maspalomas lighthouse. Covered swimming pool and gym. Wines served in the restaurant are made from grapes grown in the hotel's own vineyard.

Oficial Mayor José Rubio, 35290 San Bartolomé de Tirajana. Tel: (928) 123000.
www.hotelesinsulares.com
www.hotellastirajanas.com

Molino del Agua de Fataga★★

Rural hotel in a 200-year-old building named after the restored gofio mill which it stands next to. The restaurant serves authentic Canarian recipes.

Carretera de San Bartolomé a Fataga, km. 1, 35280 Fataga.
Tel: (928) 172089.

Princesa Guayarmina★★

Peaceful, former spa hotel surrounded by the lush flora of the Agaete Valley. Good for walking but also within easy reach of the beach, 5km away. Various health treatments on offer including acupuncture, massage and holistic health consultations.

There are two conference rooms with capacity for 25–30 people each.

Los Berrazales, 35480 Agaete, Tel: (928) 898009.

Santa Catalina★★★★

A luxury hotel opened in 1890 situated in the residential area of Ciudad Jardín. Rooms either have a sea view or overlook subtropical gardens. Many useful facilities: free parking, babysitting, a casino, 24-hour medical attention and car hire service.

León y Castillo, 227, 35005 Las Palmas. Tel: (928) 234040.
www.hotelsantacatalina.com

Rural hotel in Vega de San Mateo

TENERIFE

Costa Salada ★★★

The dining room of this small hotel has large, relaxing views over a rocky shoreline and most of the 12 rooms look out on to the ocean. Heated swimming pool, sauna, jacuzzi and golf practice area. Although the address is La Laguna, the hotel is situated between Tejina and Valle de Guerra.

Camino La Costa, Finca Oasis Valle de Guerra, 38270 La Laguna. Tel: (922) 546062.

www.costasalada.com

Gran Hotel Bahía del Duque★★★★★

Tenerife's most luxurious hotel built in imitation traditional style. Smart-casual dress expected. The hotel's restaurant, El Duque, is one of the most expensive on the island.

Alcalde Walter Paeztmann, 38670 Playa de las Américas. Tel: (922) 713000.

www.bahia-duque.com

Hotel Rural Orotava★★

Located in the historical centre of La Orotava, this 16th-century house was the home of the Marquis of la Florida whose family lived here for nine generations up to the 18th century. It has a large inner patio. There are views of the town and Mount Teide from the tower.

Calle Carrera, 17, 38300 La Orotava. Tel: (922) 322793. www.saborcanario.net

La Quinta Roja★★★★

This old house, originally the residence of the Marquis of La Quinta Roja and then used as a nunnery, stands on the town's main square. Its bar is open to the public. Mountain bikes available.

Glorieta de San Francisco, 38450 Garachico. Tel: (922) 133377.

www.quintaroja.com

Mare Nostrum Resort★★★★★

Choose between five luxury hotels all clustering around a large round swimming pool: the Mediterranean Palace, the Sir Anthony, the Julio César Palace, the Cleopatra Palace and the Marco Antonio Palace. Various games and activities on offer as well as live entertainment.

Avenida de las Americas, 38660 Arona. Tel: (922) 757545. www.expogrupo.com

Parador de las Cañadas del Teide★★★

The only building in the Cañadas del Teide national park, at over 2,000m above sea level. Some of the bedrooms have grand views of Mount Teide. The restaurant serves typical Canarian cuisine.

Las Cañadas del Teide, 38300 La Orotava. Tel: (922) 374841

www.parador.es

San Roque★★★★

An 18th-century house in an atmospheric old town that has been treated to a touch of avant garde art. Dinner and breakfast are served by the swimming pool. All rooms have flat-screen TVs, and video and DVD players (there is a library of films at reception).

Esteban de Ponte, 32, 38450 Garachico. Tel: (922) 133435.

www.hotelsanroque.com

LA GOMERA

Jardín Tecina★★★★

A hotel composed of bungalows in a terraced garden. Bedrooms have views of the garden or the sea. It has a golf course, tennis and squash courts, fitness centre, massage, several swimming pools and a diving school.

Lomada de Tecina, 38810 San Sebastián

de la Gomera. Tel: (922) 145850.
www.jardin-tecina.com
Parador Conde de la Gomera★★★
A Canary Islands mansion standing in a
garden planted with subtropical species,
decorated with maritime paraphernalia.
Great views of the ocean with Tenerife
and Mount Teide in the background.
38800 San Sebastián de la Gomera.
Tel: (922) 871100.
www.parador.es

LA PALMA
Parador de la Palma★★★
The architecture of this purpose-built
parador echoes the traditional Canarian
style. It stands in a beautiful location,
near the capital of the island and the
airport, and is surrounded by a beautiful
garden well-stocked with native plants.

Carretera de el Zumacal, 38720 Breña
Baja. Tel: (922) 435828. www.parador.es
Sol Élite La Palma★★★★
This big chain hotel is surrounded by a
banana plantation and faces the sea. It
has all the comforts, including two
pools, fitness centre, sauna, massage
room, restaurants and astronomical
observatory.
Puerto Naos, 38760 Los Llanos de
Ariadne. Tel: (922) 408000.

EL HIERRO
Parador del Hierro★★★
This modern parador stands in a
peaceful spot on the seashore facing
the Roque de Bonanza. It has wooden
balconies, white walls and an elegant
colonial décor. The rooms have sea
views. Swimming pool.
Las Playas, 15, 38900
Valverde. Tel: (922)
558036. www.parador.es
Punta Grande★
With only four
bedrooms, this claims
to be the smallest hotel
in the world. The
building is an old
customs house situated
on a solitary pier. It is
decorated with a
variety of maritime
ephemera. The rooms
are simply decorated
(without phone, TV
or minibar) and the
bathrooms incorporate
wood taken from ships.
Las Puntas, 38911
Frontera.
Tel: (922) 559081.

Los Cristianos

The adverse effects of tourism on the southern coastlines of Gran Canaria and Tenerife are well documented and well discussed. But this does not necessarily mean that lessons have been learned. In fact, the large-scale developments of Puerto Rico on Gran Canaria argue the reverse. Only La Palma enforces meaningful controls on tourism development (no advertising hoardings, no high-rise hotels, and so on).

There are, of course, many benefits to the islands and their visitors from the careful development of tourism. The debate goes something like this.

In favour of large-scale development: new roads, hotels, and apartments bring more jobs for the locals (Canarian unemployment used to be very high); new roads attract visitors to villages, so craft, souvenir and restaurant premises can thrive; work in tourism is all-year-round and is not subject to the hardship or vicissitudes of farming.

Against large-scale development: hoteliers and time-share operators bring in their own staff and exclude the locals; as young people leave their villages for tourism work, so these settlements are depopulated and die (this in itself is arguably a bad thing, but commercially it is also folly as villages also attract tourists); tourists swamp villages and irrevocably change their character; development brings pollution and destruction of flora and fauna.

Another issue is the question of what direction tourism should take in the Canaries. Do visitors really want to suffer constant haranguing from time-share touts? The obvious answer is no, and strict regulations have now been passed so that only 'legal time-share representatives' can roam the streets. The 'pile it high and sell it cheap' policy may mean more people in the short term, but the long-term risks are great. The image of the islands has already been badly damaged. While similar islands that cultivate an up-market image (such as Madeira) may perhaps have less to offer than the Canaries, they consistently attract higher-spending tourists who, in the long run, are more profitable.

Profitable operations need not resort to bland international mediocrity, as the island paradores, and such establishments as the Hotel Tecina on La Gomera prove. However, with the new building regulations for resort areas coming into force, only four- and five-star hotels will now be built, thus improving the overall image, and avoiding a bad reputation.

The narrow streets of Puerto de Mogán (left) attract many visitors, as do the beaches on southern Gran Canaria (above)

On Business

The Canary Islands are no longer the trade hub that their geographical position, halfway between Europe, Africa, and the Americas, once made them. Trade routes have changed, and ships which once stopped here for refuelling and 'rest and recreation' can now sail by, or they have been replaced with air travel, and more fashionable destinations.

Offices on Plaza de España, Santa Cruz

The island's only business cities are the provincial capitals of Las Palmas and Santa Cruz de Tenerife. Both rely heavily on oil-refining. Santa Cruz is one of the largest refiners in all Spain, processing Venezuelan crude oil for domestic use. In terms of international trade and commerce, Las Palmas is much more important than Santa Cruz, attracting around 8,000 ships a year. Around five million tons of freight (mostly oil and petroleum) flow in, and one million tons of foodstuffs are exported, mostly to the Spanish mainland.

As part of Spain and therefore a member of the European Union, the islands enforce EU trading conditions. If you require information on any aspect of trading in the Canaries before you depart, contact the Spanish Commercial Office at 66 Chiltern Street, London W1U 4LS (telephone requests are not dealt with) or see www.icex.es. For background on the economic development of the Canary Islands see the website of the Sociedad para el Desarrollo Económico de Canarias www.sodecan.es and for statistics, www.istac.rcanaria.es. Another useful source of information, for Gran Canaria, is the Sociedad de Promoción Económica de Gran Canaria www.investingrancanaria.com.

Business Etiquette

Canarians are generally friendly, easy-going people who will often suggest talking business over a slap-up lunch. Don't think this is wasted time or effort. Life is slower here in most aspects than on mainland Europe (although Las Palmas on Gran Canaria is an exception), but don't take this as a sign of provincial naïvety. Many successful businessmen have moved from mainland Spain to the Canaries to facilitate or oversee their import-export trades, and have a keen eye for the next business opportunity.

Business Services

Tenerife and Gran Canaria have sizeable expatriate communities (mostly English, but also German and Scandinavian), who supply and use business services. Pick up any of the English-language publications (*see Media, p182*) and you will find advertisements for office equipment, secretarial, translation and interpretation services, removals and freight, messengers, and all manner of insurance and financial brokers.

If you are planning to set up your own business on the islands, or to take any legal or financial advice, be very careful. As one of the advertisements frankly admits, 'it's a minefield!'.

Two useful publications might be *You and the Law in Spain* by David Searl, published by Santana (*www.santanabooks.com*), and the booklet *Doing Business in Spain* published by the Spanish Chamber of Commerce in Britain.

Conferences

For somewhere intimate to get ideas thrashed out in workgroups, a hotel on a smaller island may be best. The Parador on La Gomera is a perfect venue, with little to distract delegates from serious business. Another choice on the island is the excellent Hotel Jardín Tecina (*see p168*). The only hotel that a business conference organiser would consider on La Palma, meanwhile, is the Sol Élite La Palma at Puerto Naos (*see p169*). Going to the extreme, the Parador on El Hierro is about as far away as you can get from workaday routine. (For information on the *paradors, see pp163–4*).

For larger groups and younger sales teams, a resort on Gran Canaria or Tenerife might be a better choice and there are many hotels catering for business meetings, although not all will have sophisticated sound and light facilities for presentations. Playa de las Américas has several hotels with convention halls. Chief among these is the luxurious Mare Nostrum complex, part of Expo Grupo (*see p168*). Maspalomas is also a good place for a serious conference with its smart hotels and its purpose-built conference centre, the **Palacio de Congresos de Maspalomas** (*Tel: (928) 128000. www.maspalomas-congresos.com*), holding 5,000 people.

Las Palmas de Gran Canaria is also geared up for conferences with some impressive four- and five-star hotels. Its pride is the Palacio de Congresos de Canarias. *For information contact Las Palmas Convention Bureau Tel: (928) 446829. www.laspalmasgccb.com*

Santa Cruz de Tenerife is less well provided for, but a halfway house on the island between big city and brash resort is Puerto de la Cruz, which has some traditional class but plenty of modern amenities too. For more information see the Tenerife Convention Bureau website, *www.tenerifecb.com*

Hotel groups catering for business clients in the Canary Islands include the following:
Atlantia *Tel: (902) 100988 www.aacanarias.com*
NH *Tel: (902) 115116 www.nhhotels.com*
Sol Melia *Tel: (902) 144444 www.solmelia.com*
H10 *Tel: (902) 100906 www.h10.es*
Husa *Tel: (902) 100710 www.husa.es*

Congenial surroundings for a business meeting

Practical Guide

Arriving
Visitors from EU countries, the USA, and Canada, need only a passport to enter the Canary Islands. A residence permit or special visa is necessary for stays longer than 90 days.

By Air
Gran Canaria's airport is located on the east coast midway between Maspalomas and Las Palmas. Tenerife has two airports: **Tenerife Norte** (North, also called Los Rodeos) serving Santa Cruz, La Laguna and Puerto de la Cruz and **Tenerife Sur** (South, also called Reina Sofía) for the southern resorts. The three small islands also have airports. For information see *www.aena.es*

Spain's national airline is **Iberia** (*Tel: (902) 400500. www.iberia.com*). **Air Europa** (*Tel: (907) 401501 www.air-europa.com*) and **Spanair** (*Tel: (902) 131415 www.spanair.es*) also fly between mainland Spain and the Canary Islands.

Regular airport buses go from: Gran Canaria airport to Las Palmas and Maspalomas; from Tenerife South to Los Cristianos/Playa de las Américas/Santa Cruz, and from Tenerife North to Puerto de la Cruz and Santa Cruz. There are also express buses that link Tenerife's two airports. Regular local bus services also run from other island airports. All airports have taxis to meet inter-island flights.

By Boat
Trasmediterránea ships (*Tel: (902) 454645 www.trasmediterranea.es*) sail from Cádiz on mainland Spain to Las Palmas de Gran Canaria and Santa Cruz de Tenerife.

Camping
Given the scarcity of good, cheap accommodation on the islands, this is one of the few budget options. There are few official campsites, but most have good facilities (*see pp164–5*).

Children
The more popular Canary Islands are completely geared for family holidays, and within the major resorts you will find all you need in the way of baby care products. Babysitters can be found for older children, and many hotels have specific children's activities and 'clubs'.

Climate
For all-year-round sunshine you'll have to go to the south of Gran Canaria or the south of Tenerife. The small westerly islands can be quite cool, though for most of the winter they are pleasantly spring-like to North Europeans.

If you're visiting the north of the larger islands, be prepared for some rain and cooler temperatures in the winter. Winds can also be strong. Summer sunshine is virtually guaranteed everywhere.

Consulates
Most Western countries have a consulate in the Canary Islands. They include:
Ireland *Castillo 8-4A, Santa Cruz de Tenerife. Tel: (922) 245671.*
UK *Plaza de Weyler 8, Santa Cruz de Tenerife. Tel: (922) 286863; Edificio*

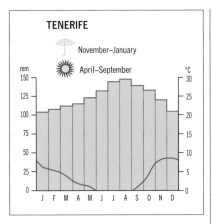

TENERIFE

☂ November–January

☀ April–September

Weather Conversion Chart
25.4mm = 1 inch
°F = 1.8 x °C + 32

Conversion Table		
FROM	TO	MULTIPLY BY
Inches	Centimetres	2.54
Feet	Metres	0.3048
Yards	Metres	0.9144
Miles	Kilometres	1.6090
Acres	Hectares	0.4047
Gallons	Litres	4.5460
Ounces	Grams	28.35
Pounds	Grams	453.6
Pounds	Kilograms	0.4536
Tons	Tonnes	1.0160

To convert back, for example from centimetres to inches, divide by the number in the third column.

Cataluña, Calle de Luis Morote, 6, 35007, Las Palmas, Gran Canaria.
Tel: (928) 262508.
USA *Calle Martínez de Escobar, 3, Las Palmas, Gran Canaria. Tel: (928) 222552.*

Crime

Theft from cars is the most common form of crime against tourists on the islands, with handbag-snatching a close second. Never leave anything of value in your car, and make sure it is locked at all times. In contrast to Las Palmas, other Canarian towns and villages are quite safe. However, when walking in tourist areas, carry handbags on the side away from the road, and be vigilant.

Hotels usually have safes for hire, although hotel staff are honest and break-ins at good hotels are rare. Apartments are less easy to police.

Violence against tourists is unusual,

Men's Suits

UK	36	38	40	42	44	46	48
Rest of Europe	46	48	50	52	54	56	58
US	36	38	40	42	44	46	48

Dress Sizes

UK	8	10	12	14	16	18
France	36	38	40	42	44	46
Italy	38	40	42	44	46	48
Rest of Europe	34	36	38	40	42	44
US	6	8	10	12	14	16

Men's Shirts

UK	14	14.5	15	15.5	16	16.5	17
Rest of Europe	36	37	38	39/40	41	42	43
US	14	14.5	15	15.5	16	16.5	17

Men's Shoes

UK	7	7.5	8.5	9.5	10.5	11
Rest of Europe	41	42	43	44	45	46
US	8	8.5	9.5	10.5	11.5	12

Women's Shoes

UK	4.5	5	5.5	6	6.5	7
Rest of Europe	38	38	39	39	40	41
US	6	6.5	7	7.5	8	8.5

Ferries operate regularly to and from the islands

but don't tempt fate by treading the seamier streets of Las Palmas after dark.

If you are a victim of robbery, report the incident to the local police who will give you a copy of your statement for insurance purpose.

Customs Regulations

For customs purposes the Canary Islands are not members of the EU. The duty-free allowance for goods taken in or out (applicable to persons 17 and over) include: 2 litres of wine; 1 litre of spirits; 200 cigarettes (or 100 *cigarillos* or 50 cigars or 250g tobacco); 60cc perfume or 250cc toilet water; €145 worth of gifts per person.

Driving
Car Hire

It is possible to take your own car to the islands via mainland Spain, but as the Canary Islands provide very reasonable car hire rates, it hardly seems worth the effort or expense.

Reserving a hire car when you book your flights is often the cheapest option. The big multinational car hire companies are represented in the Canary Islands, although you will get a better deal by using a local company such as *Cicar* (Canary Island Car *Tel: (902) 244444 www.cicar.com*) which has a comprehensive network of offices, **Autoreisen** (*Tel: (928) 574744*) or **Niza Cars** (*Tel: (922) 792919 www.nizacars.com*).

Documentation

All British, European, American and Australian driving licences are valid, although it may be advisable to take a Spanish translation with you (contact a motoring organisation in your own country before travelling). An

International Driving Permit is not necessary.

Petrol

Petrol stations are relatively common along the main roads, with 24-hour opening in the larger resorts and towns; but don't drive into the mountains on a near-empty tank, as there are often long and winding stretches of road without anywhere to fill up.

Rules of the Road

Driving is on the right. Seat belts are compulsory in the front and the back and you must have a yellow reflective waistcoat in the passenger compartment in case of a breakdown. Children under 12 must travel in the back of the car. In towns cars must be parked facing the direction of the movement of traffic.

The standard of roads is surprisingly high, with many newly built and very smoothly surfaced. Motorways (*autopistas*) run along the north and east coast of Tenerife and the east coast of Gran Canaria, connecting airports with major resorts in 30 minutes or less.

The standard of driving is reasonable, although beware of oncoming traffic (particularly tour coaches) and impatient drivers on hairpin bends in mountainous areas. Beware of traffic jams in Las Palmas (Gran Canaria), Puerto de la Cruz and Santa Cruz (Tenerife). Street parking is also very difficult in these towns (Las Palmas is particularly bad) and it is usually best to find an underground car park. Beware

Watch out for hazards near Mount Teide!

Hairpin bends in the Valle Gran Rey

the fiendish one-way systems in Las Palmas and Puerto de la Cruz (whose town centre is notoriously difficult to negotiate).

Electricity

The current throughout the islands is 220 volts AC, and sockets take the circular two-pin continental-style plug.

Emergency Telephone Numbers

General: 112
Police (*Policia Nacional*): 091
Ambulance: 061
Fire: 080
Emergencies at sea: 900 202202

Health

No vaccinations are necessary for a visit to the Canary Islands.

EU citizens can obtain a refund of most medical costs by using form E111 (available from post offices and Health or Social Security offices) although this is being replaced by the European Health Insurance Card (EHIC) which entitles the holder to the same treatment as a Spanish national. It may still be advisable to take out private medical insurance.

The most common complaints are stomach upsets caused by a sudden change of diet and too much sun. Break yourself in gradually to sunbathing and always use suntan lotions and blocks. Remember that children are particularly vulnerable.

There are many English-speaking dentists and doctors. Ask your hotel or tourist information office for the nearest one. Minor ailments can usually be treated at the chemist (*farmacia*). At least one chemist per town or area stays open after hours. Its location is posted in the window of all the other chemists (also in the tourist office and local newspaper).

Hitchhiking

This is legal, though not totally safe if you are alone, and with the large number of North European holiday drivers on the roads not likely to be a quick way of getting around. An official hitchhiker's card (obtainable from Youth Hostel Associations) may help.

Lost Property

Lost property offices are few and far between. Ask the tourist office where to go locally. Report lost valuables to the Municipal Police or Guardia Civil and obtain a form for your own holiday insurance purposes.

Maps

It is surprisingly difficult to find good maps of the Canary Islands even on the islands themselves. Car hire companies and the island tourist offices give out maps which are enough to get around with, but are not sufficient for exploring off the beaten track or to use for hiking.

The best source of maps for walking is

Take special care on mountain roads such as this in the Llano de Ucanca

LANGUAGE

Canary Islanders speak Spanish, or to be more accurate Castilian (the language of most of mainland Spain). The only real difference that the non-language student will notice is that the letter **c** and **z** are pronounced (softly), instead of lisped with a 'th' sound.

There are a few indigenous words still in use, the most notable being **papa(s)** for potato(es) and **guagua** (pronounced wah-wah) for bus.

It's quite possible in some major resorts to get through two weeks on the islands speaking, and even hearing, nothing other than English. However, off the beaten track, and particularly on the smaller islands, a smattering of Spanish will be helpful if not essential. But wherever you are, your attempts to master a few phrases and, at the very least, daily greetings will always be appreciated.

PRONUNCIATION

Try to remember the following basic rules:

Consonants

c is soft before e and i (eg, Barcelona), but hard at any other time – **como**? (pardon?) pronounced 'ko-mo'.

g at the start of a word is a hard sound (as in get). In the middle of a word it is like the throaty 'ch' as in the Scottish 'loch' – **urgencia** (emergency) is pronounced 'ooer-chensee-ah'. In **agua** (water) it is hardly pronounced at all ('ah-kwa').

h is always silent – **hospital** is pronounced 'ospitahl'.

j is also pronounced like the ch in 'loch' – **jamón** (ham) is pronounced 'ch-amon'.

ll is always like 'll' in million – **lleno** (full) is pronounced 'lyay-no'.

ñ is like 'ni' in onion – **España** (Spain) is pronounced 'ay-spanya'.

qu is like k in key – **quánto**? (how much?) is pronounced 'kwan-toe'.

r is rolled: **rr** is rolled even harder.

v is like b in bottle – **vino** (wine) is pronounced 'bee-no'.

x is like s – **excelente** (excellent) is pronounced 'ess-say-len-tay'.

Vowels

a is a short 'ah' sound – **gracias** (thank you). It is never long as in the English 'gracious'. All the other vowels are long sounds. The letter **e** is a cross between the short English e (as in get) and the long English **a** (as in grace) – **de** (of/from) is pronounced 'day' but in a clipped way. The letter **i** is a long 'ee' sound as in sí (yes), pronounced 'see', and **u** is like 'oo' in boot – **una** (one). The letter **o** is an 'oh' sound.

DAYS OF THE WEEK	
Sunday	domingo
Monday	lunes
Tuesday	martes
Wednesday	miércoles
Thursday	jueves
Friday	viernes
Saturday	sábado

USEFUL WORDS AND PHRASES

yes/no	sí/no
hello	hola
good morning	buenos días
good afternoon	buenas tardes
goodnight	buenas noches
goodbye	adiós
please	por favor
thank you	gracias
you're welcome	de nada
today	hoy
tomorrow	mañana
yesterday	ayer
I am English	Soy inglés
do you speak English?	¿habla inglés? (informal) ¿habla usted inglés? (formal)
very well/good	muy bien/vale
where is . . ?	¿dónde está . . ?
what/when	qué/cuándo
why/how	por qué/cómo
how much is . . ?	¿cuánto vale/cuesta . . ?
here/there	aquí/ahí
open/closed	abierto/cerrado
right, left	derecho/a, izquierdo/a
sorry!	¡lo siento!
excuse me (can I get past?)	perdóneme
(can you help?)	por favor –
sir, madam, miss	señor, señora, señorita
I don't understand	no comprendo
I would like . . .	quiero/quisiera . . .
large/small	grande/pequeño
do you have . . ?	¿tiene . . ?
please write it down	por favor, escríbalo

NUMBERS

0	cero
1	uno/a
2	dos
3	tres
4	cuatro
5	cinco
6	seis
7	siete
8	ocho
9	nueve
10	diez
11	once
12	doce
13	trece
14	catorce
15	quince
16	dieciséis
17	diecisiete
18	dieciocho
19	diecinueve
20	veinte
21	veintiuno
30	treinta
40	cuarenta
50	cincuenta
60	sesenta
70	setenta
80	ochenta
90	noventa
100	cien/ciento/a
101	ciento uno/a
200	doscientos/as
500	quinientos/as
1000	mil
2000	dos mil
1,000,000	un millón

Servicio de Publicaciones del Instituto Geográfico Nacional, *General Ibañez de Ibero, 3, 28003 Madrid. Tel: (91) 597 9684. www.cnig.es*

Media

All the major international papers are available in the large towns and popular resorts, usually the day after publication. There are several newspapers and magazines written for the English-speaking visitor to the Canary Islands. Gran Canaria has surprisingly little. In Tenerife look out for the *Tenerife News*. For Spanish speakers, *La Gaceta de Canarias* and *Diario de Avisos* include useful local listings.

Money Matters

The euro (€) is the unit of currency used in the islands. There are seven denominations of the euro note: €5, €10, €20, €50, €100, €200 and €500; eight denominations of coins: 1 cent,

Tobacconist in Tenerife

2 cents, 5 cents, 10 cents, 20 cents, 50 cents, and €1 and €2.

Banks are generally open weekdays 9am–2pm, 9am–1pm on Saturdays (closed on Saturdays from 1 June to 31 October). A commission is always charged for changing money, and you will need your passport. Outside banking hours many travel agents and various *bureaux de change* (look for the *cambio* sign) will exchange money, but always at a lower rate than the bank. Even if the rates on display seem attractive, the deductions which they fail to advertise will cost you dearly (tourist shops are the worst culprits). Most hotels will also change money.

Opening Hours

Shops are open Monday to Saturday 9am–1pm and 4pm or 5pm to 7pm or 8pm (chemists usually close on Saturday afternoon except for the one duty chemist in each area, which is open for 24 hours). Aside from major tourist resorts, shops are closed on Sunday. Museum opening hours are variable; some close on Sunday, others on a Monday (or another weekday), while some remain open all week. Church hours also vary, but they are sure to be open for morning or evening services.

Places of Worship

Catholic Mass is celebrated in various languages in the major resorts throughout the islands (details from the tourist office, the local newspapers, or on church notice boards).

There are Anglican churches at Ciudad Jardín, Las Palmas on Gran Canaria and on Tenerife at Taoro Park,

Puerto de la Cruz and in the Pueblo Canario in Playa de las Américas. Evangelical services take place in Tenerife Christian Centre in Puerto de la Cruz. The Ecumenical Church in Playa del Inglés (Gran Canaria) is used by several denominations. There is a synagogue in Calle Remedios, Las Palmas.

Police
Police responsibilities are split between the Policía Municipal (blue uniform and cap) who direct traffic and have other municipal duties; the Policía Nacional (brown uniform and beret) who are in charge of crime in the towns; the Guardia Civil (pea-green uniform and cap) who look after crime and patrol the highways in rural areas.

Postal Services
Post offices are open weekdays 9am–2pm and 9am–1pm on Saturday. Stamps (*sellos* or *timbres*) can also be bought at tobacconists called estancos and marked with a 'T' sign. Postboxes are painted yellow. If there are two slots, use the one marked *extranjeros* (foreign) for postcards home.

Public Holidays
1 January New Year's Day
6 January Epiphany
1 May Labour Day
15 August Assumption
12 October Columbus Day
1 November All Saints' Day
6 December Constitution Day
8 December Immaculate Conception
25 December Christmas Day
Moveable feasts are Maundy Thursday

and Good Friday. In addition to these, there are several local feast days.

Public Transport
Air
Binter airlines (*Tel: (902) 391392. www.bintercanarias.es*) flies hourly at peak times between Tenerife Norte and Gran Canaria. Regular services link all the islands. **Isla Airways** (*Tel: (902) 477478 www.islasairways.com*) also has several flights a day between Tenerife and Gran Canaria and also connects Tenerife Norte with the island of La Palma.

A typical public phone box

Buses

Bus services (buses are known as *guaguas*) on Gran Canaria and Tenerife are fast and reliable. The smaller islands are less well served. If you intend travelling a lot on buses, consider a *bono* (literally, a voucher) which for a reasonable annual amount entitles you to buy tickets at about 30 per cent less (available from main bus stations).

For bus information on Tenerife *Tel: (922) 479500* or see *www.titsa.com*; for Gran Canaria *Tel: (902) 381110* or see *www.globalsu.net*. For the other islands, ask at the tourist information office.

Ferries

The Norwegian company **Fred Olsen** (*Tel: (902) 100107 www.fredolsen.es*), established in the Canary Islands for over a century, operates high speed services between Agaete on Gran Canaria and Santa Cruz de Tenerife. From Los Cristianos in southern Tenerife its ferries go to La Gomera, La Palma and El Hierro. **Naviera Armas** (*Tel: (902) 456500 www.naviera-armas.com*) sails from Santa Cruz de Tenerife to Las Palmas (3 hours 15 minutes) and La Palma (a six-hour trip). From Los Cristianos it sails to San Sebastian (La Gomera) and Valverde (El Hierro).

Taxis

These are recognisable by a green light in the windscreen or on a white roof and an official plate with the letters SP, standing for *servicio público* (public service). The light shows *libre* (free) when they are available for hire. For short trips within tourist areas many cabbies won't bother to put their meters on, though you will rarely be cheated. Boards by the main taxi ranks display fixed prices between the most popular destinations. For longer distances confirm the price before you start.

Students and Youth Travel

For various reasons the Canary Islands do not attract the backpacking youngsters seen in many other holiday islands throughout the world. There are some official camping sites and no youth hostels.

Telephones

You can make international calls from virtually any phone on the islands. Hotels usually levy a hefty surcharge for phone calls. Calls are cheaper after 8pm. For international calls, dial 00, wait for the tone to indicate that you have a line, then dial your country code (Australia 61, Canada and the USA 1, Ireland 353, UK 44), followed by the local code (omitting the first 0), then the number.

All the Canary Islands' telephone numbers consist of nine digits. Those within the province of Las Palmas (Gran Canaria, Fuerteventura, and Lanzarote) start with 928, and those within the Santa Cruz de Tenerife province (Tenerife, La Gomera, La Palma, and El Hierro) begin with 922. The nine digits must be dialled for all calls, including local ones.

Time

The Canaries maintain Greenwich Mean Time in the winter, which is one hour behind most European countries and in line with the UK. The clocks go forward one hour in summer. The Canaries are five hours ahead of US Eastern Standard Time, and eight hours ahead of Pacific Time. Johannesburg is ahead by one hour, Australia by 10 hours, and New Zealand by 12 hours.

Tipping

Most hotels and some restaurant bills include a service charge. A small tip (around 10 per cent) for a well-served meal, a friendly taxi driver, or hotel staff who have been particularly helpful, will be appreciated. Don't forget to leave the hotel maid something, too.

Toilets

Public toilets are very clean and recommendable, with beach areas having in most cases a public (free) shower on the beach, and private showers/toilet facilities for a small fee. In order of preference, use those in hotels, restaurants and bars. Buy a drink in the latter as a matter of courtesy.

There are several terms for toilets: *servicios, aseos, WC, retretes*. The doors are usually marked *Señoras* (ladies) and *Caballeros* (gentlemen).

Tourist Information

Responsibilities for tourist information have been devolved by the Spanish government to the regions and the Spanish national tourist offices abroad will only be able to give you very general information. Almost all of it is on the website *www.spaininfo.com* or *www.tourspain.co.uk*

Much better is to direct your enquiry to the island(s) you are going to visit.

Buses are quick and reliable in the Canary Islands

Each has its own website:
Gran Canaria: *www.grancanaria.com*
Tenerife: *www.webtenerife.com* and
www.puntoinfo.idecnet.com
La Gomera: *www.gomera-island.com*
La Palma: *www.lapalmaturismo.com*
El Hierro: *www.el-hierro.org*

Almost every town of any size has its own tourist information office dispensing free maps and leaflets and advising on public transport and local events. All offices should have at least one English-speaking member of staff and be able to advise you on accommodation.

Travellers with Disabilities
There are wheelchair facilities at all the international terminals, and as hotels and apartments continue to be built, so more choice becomes available for the wheelchair user.

Most of the wheelchair-equipped places to stay are in the newer resorts of

Popular taxi journeys are given fixed prices

Playa del Inglés on Gran Canaria, and Playa de las Américas on Tenerife. Another possibility is Puerto de la Cruz on Tenerife, which offers several wheelchair-friendly hotels.

Tenerife has a purpose-built centre for the disabled holidaymaker, the Mar y Sol resort in Los Cristianos. For information about it, *Tel: (922) 750540* or, in the UK, contact: **ATS Travel**, *1 Tank Lane Road, Purfleet, Essex. Tel: (01708) 863198. www.assistedholidays.com*

General facilities throughout the islands, however, are poor to non-existent. There are very few adapted toilets, adapted public transport facilities, or adapted hire cars (even automatics are rare). Kerbs are high and the terrain is often steep.

The Spanish association for disabled travellers is **Federación ECOM**, *Gran Vía de les Corts Catalanes, 562-2a, 08011 Barcelona. Tel: (93) 451 55 50. www.ecom.es.* Another useful organisation is **COCEMFE** (Confederación Coordinadora Estatal de Minusvalidos Físicos De España) *Calle Luis Cabrera 63, 28002 Madrid. Tel: (91) 744 36 00. www.cocemfe.es.* UK travellers can also contact the **Holiday Care Service** for their special fact sheets on Gran Canaria, Lanzarote, and Tenerife, and for any general advice: *7th Floor, Sunley House 4 Bedford Park, Croydon, Surrey CR0 2AP. Tel: (0845) 124 9971* (or from outside the UK: *(+ 44) 208 760 0072*). *www.holidaycare.org.uk.* The Royal Association for Disability and Rehabilitation (**RADAR** *Tel: (0171) 250 3222*), publishes a guide to travel abroad which includes information on the Canary Islands.

MAKE A DIFFERENCE WHEN YOU TRAVEL

The Travel Foundation is a UK charity that cares for the places we love to visit.

By following this simple advice, you can get more out of your holiday – and help make a positive difference to the lives of the people and places you visit. You can also help to ensure there are special places for us all to visit – for generations to come!

To find out more about The Travel Foundation and what you can do, please visit *www.thetravelfoundation.org.uk*.

What you can do:

- Remove any packaging from items (and recycle if possible) before you go on holiday.
- Booking excursions that use local suppliers or using local guides and taxis will enrich your holiday experience and help support the local economy.
- Hire a car only if you need to. Using public transport, bicycles and walking are environmentally-friendlier alternatives.
- Respect local culture and traditions. Ensure your dress and behaviour is appropriate for the places you visit. Ask permission before taking photographs of people or their homes.
- Turn down/off heating or air conditioning when not required.

Switch off lights and turn the television off rather than leave on standby.

- Please don't have your photograph taken with any 'wild' animals (such as lion or tiger cubs, chimpanzees or exotic birds). They are taken from the wild when young, often mistreated and killed when too big or difficult to handle.
- Do use water sparingly. Take showers instead of baths and inform staff if you are happy to re-use towels and bed linen rather than replace daily.
- Please don't pick flowers and plants or collect pebbles, seashells, coral or starfish. Leave them for others to enjoy.
- Please don't buy products made from endangered plants or animals, including hardwoods, ivory, corals, reptiles or turtles. If in doubt – don't buy.
- Do buy locally-made products – shopping in locally-owned outlets and treating yourself to local food and drink is a great way to get into the holiday spirit and benefits local families.
- Coral is extremely fragile. Please don't step on or remove it and avoid kicking up sand.

ACKNOWLEDGEMENTS

Thomas Cook wishes to thank the following photographers, libraries and other organisations for their assistance in the preparation of this book, and to whom the copyright belongs.

CAROLINE JONES 83

JONATHAN SMITH 1, 2, 4, 6, 7, 8, 9, 10, 11, 13, 14, 15, 16, 17, 18, 19, 20, 21, 23, 24. 25. 28. 30, 31, 32, 33, 34, 35, 36, 38, 39, 40, 41, 42, 43, 44, 45, 46, 48, 49, 50, 51, 52, 53, 54, 55, 56, 57, 58, 59, 60, 66, 68, 69, 70, 71, 73, 75, 76, 77, 79, 80, 81, 82, 84, 85, 87, 88, 89, 90, 91, 93, 94, 95, 96, 97, 99, 100, 101, 102, 103, 104, 105, 106, 108, 109, 110, 111, 112, 114, 115, 132, 134, 135, 136, 137, 138, 139, 140, 141, 142, 143, 144, 145, 146, 147, 148, 149, 150, 153, 154, 155, 156, 157, 158, 159, 161, 162, 163, 165, 167, 169, 170, 171, 172, 173, 176, 177, 178, 179, 182, 183, 185, 186

MARY EVANS PICTURE LIBRARY 62

PICTURES COLOUR LIBRARY 123b, 126, 128a, 128b, 131

THOMAS COOK TOUR OPERATIONS LTD 116a, 116b, 118, 119, 120, 121, 122, 123a, 124, 125

Index: INDEXING SPECIALISTS

Copy-editing: CATHERINE BURCH for CAMBRIDGE PUBLISHING MANAGEMENT LTD

Proofreading: RICHARD HALL for CAMBRIDGE PUBLISHING MANAGEMENT LTD

Travellers **Gran Canaria & Tenerife**

Feedback Form

Please help us improve future editions by taking part in our reader survey. Every returned form will be acknowledged. To show our appreciation we will send you a voucher entitling you to £1 off your next *Travellers* guide or any other Thomas Cook guidebook ordered direct from Thomas Cook Publishing. Just take a few minutes to complete and return this form to us.

We'd also be glad to hear of your comments, updates or recommendations on places we cover or you think that we ought to cover.

1. Which of the following tempted you into buying your *Travellers* guide:
   (Please tick as many as appropriate)

   a) the price ☐

   b) the cover ☐

   c) the content ☐

   d) other _____

2. What do you think of:

   a) the cover design _____

   b) the design and layout styles within the book _____

   c) the content_____

   d) the maps _____

3. Please tell us about any features that in your opinion could be changed, improved or added in future editions of the book or any other comments you would like to make concerning this book _____

   _____

   _____

   _____

   _____

4. What is the single most useful/helpful aspect of this book?_____

   _____

cut along the dotted line

5. Have you purchased other *Travellers* guides in the series?

a) yes   ☐

b) no   ☐

If yes, please specify which titles _____

6. Would you purchase other *Travellers* guides?

a) yes   ☐

b) no   ☐

If no, please specify why not _____

Your age category: ☐ under 21   ☐ 21–30   ☐ 31–40   ☐ 41–50   ☐ 51+

Mr/Mrs/Miss/Ms/Other

Surname_____ Initials_____

Full address (please include postal or zip code):_____

_____

_____

Daytime telephone number: _____

E-mail address:_____

Please detach this page and send it to: **The Series Editor, *Travellers* guides, Thomas Cook Publishing, PO Box 227, The Thomas Cook Business Park, Units 15–16, Coningsby Road, Peterborough PE3 8SB, United Kingdom.**

Alternatively, you can e-mail us at: *books@thomascook.com*